William Mason, E. S Hoadly

A Method for the Piano-Forte

William Mason, E. S Hoadly

A Method for the Piano-Forte

ISBN/EAN: 9783744793230

Printed in Europe, USA, Canada, Australia, Japan

Cover: Foto ©Thomas Meinert / pixelio.de

More available books at **www.hansebooks.com**

A METHOD

FOR THE

PIANO-FORTE,

BY

WILLIAM MASON AND E. S. HOADLY.

American Fingering.

(An Edition of this work is published with European Fingering.)

BOSTON:
Published by OLIVER DITSON & CO., 277 Washington Street.
NEW YORK: C. H. DITSON & CO.

PREFACE.

THIS book is designed not only for those who wish to play the Piano-forte merely as an accomplishment, but also for such as intend to become its masters. It opens the shortest possible road to that proficiency which those of the former class generally desire, namely, sufficient to enable them to play ordinary accompaniments of vocal music and easy pieces at sight; to play difficult pieces with a reasonable amount of practice; and to improvise correctly, though simply, as occasion may require. At the same time it teaches thoroughly and artistically, within its limits. The training of those who aim at but moderate accomplishment should be identical with that of the professional musician, in the earlier stages of his course.

This method will be found to vary in important respects from others. It is the result of very careful and considerable experience in teaching, and of unusual opportunities for observing and closely studying the modes adopted by many of the most eminent teachers in the world. Though so much will be found that is new, there is nothing which has not been most thoroughly tested by extensive use, and of which the practical value has not been abundantly proved.

It is believed that some of the features which are original in this work are of great importance, as tending in an eminent degree to excite and retain an active interest on the part of the pupil, and to secure the most rapid, and, at the same time, thorough and accurate progress possible.

Attention is called to the following points:

1. Those explanations and minute directions which the best teachers give orally to their pupils, have, as far as possible, been written in detail; the explanations are arranged in paragraphs, and, for convenience in reference, are numbered from the beginning onward.

2. The art of fingering is more fully taught than in any previous work; new modes of overcoming difficulties are introduced, and principles are elucidated by copious analyses which enable the learner to understand them easily. Lessons are given to be fingered by the pupil, and submitted to the teacher for correction. This is a field that needs cultivation, and in which much may be done.

3. The pupil is taught to recognize intervals, and to select scales and chords mechanically upon the key-board, and thus gains a clear understanding of them with very little use of technicalities.

4. In all the exercises and recreations, before the Major scales are learned, and a good degree of finger-skill is acquired, the hand, though in different places upon the key-board, takes five-key positions only, and is not in any instance required to play double-tones or repeated-tones. Experience shows, that until a certain proficiency is attained, extensions and contractions confuse the learner, and tend to prevent the formation of a most important habit, which, in a majority of cases, assists the player; namely, the taking a five-finger position whenever the hand is placed upon the key-board. It is found also that, at first, the use of double-tones—two keys struck simultaneously by one hand, and repeated-tones—produced by striking a key successively with the same finger, tends to stiffen the muscles. These obstacles in the path of the learner are therefore excluded from the earlier lessons.

5. A new and peculiar mode of treating Accents as a means of training the pupil is introduced. Teachers can appreciate the importance of this only by large experience in its use. The Accent Exercises have been composed upon the principle that every power of the hand may be put in requisition in Piano-forte playing, and that a systematic and methodic training of all the fingers in every possible order of succession will best develop, strengthen, and fit them for use. These exercises are important, also, because they tend to discipline the mind, and impart a clear insight into divisions of time, thereby assisting the pupil to an animated style of playing, and relieving monotony.

6. The exercises are condensed as much as possible, without destroying their clearness and utility. Thus, for example, pages 102 and 103, upon Double Thirds, contain all that is valuable in a dozen pages as usually presented. By this means, a great number of exercises are introduced in a small compass, rendering the work more complete and useful.

7. While a thorough training of the hand, preparatory to encountering the difficulties of modern compositions, is going forward, a large number of Recreations and Pieces are provided to be progressively used, furnishing the pupil musical reading and culture, as well as relief. This selection of music is very pleasing; not a single composition has been admitted that is not really attractive. It affords the great advantage of studying the different styles of many eminent composers.

8. The book is divided into two Departments, Practical and Theoretical, each of which is systematically arranged, so that teachers can easily select what pupils require. This is believed to be better than such a mingling of exercises, theoretical instruction, and pieces, as might be exactly adapted to one pupil but not to others.

If pupils are trained in strict accordance with the directions here given, and do not waste their time and derange their hands by frequent indulgence in attempts to play very rapidly such music as is beyond their power of execution, they will, in much less time than has hitherto been found necessary, become really good players,—able to interpret properly the works of the great composers. They will also be saved the bitter experience of many, who, after years of familiarity with the Piano-forte, and the attainment of great supposed proficiency, apply to artistic teachers for finishing lessons, and then discover, with intense mortification, that all their habits in the use of the instrument are bad; that they have had no correct ideas upon the subject, and no foundation for good playing; in fact, cannot play the simplest passage perfectly; and that artistic playing involves, for them, an entire and well nigh impossible reformation.

PRACTICAL DEPARTMENT.

INTRODUCTION.

§ 1. *False and True Methods of Teaching the Piano Forte.*—Various standards of excellence, different degrees of attainment, and modes of training quite dissimilar, exist among teachers of the Piano Forte. Some, caring less for real accomplishment than for the show of it in their pupils, give them, in quick succession, without adequate preparation or careful training, a great number of difficult pieces; flattering them with assurances that they "play splendidly," when, in truth, mechanical accuracy is sacrificed to a hurried scrambling over the keys; expression is wholly neglected, and the apparent proficiency is owing to the fact that difficulties are avoided rather than overcome. Parents, friends, and even pupils themselves, are often entirely deceived by such management, and fully believe that great skill in the art of music is acquired, when, really, a superficial knowledge of a few pieces only is all that is gained. Other instructors, having a high regard for mechanical accuracy, with but little musical sensibility or true appreciation of the beautiful, train their pupils to execute correctly, perhaps, but allow them to do it with stiff hands, in a style which may be described as pounding, and is entirely destitute of sweetness.

But the training of true teachers, who, having high culture and fine musical sensibility, appreciate the beauties of Piano Forte music, and regard mechanical accuracy as indispensable in its performance, is thorough, careful, and patient; assisting learners to overcome difficulties and encouraging them to persevere in efforts to acquire the utmost control over their fingers and hands; giving them exercises and pieces for practice, selected with special reference to their most rapid progress, urging them to play even the most simple music as perfectly as possible; to listen to their own performances and enjoy them; to give the closest attention and study to the true expression of every passage; to discriminate between different styles of composition; to form taste upon true models; to cultivate mind as well as fingers, and so to become refined and elevated by study and practice. Pupils so trained are able to interpret properly the works of great composers; playing, now softly, then powerfully; in some passages with liquid sweetness and delicacy, in others, with the greatest animation and brilliancy; in all, with that soul-moving expression which charms and enraptures those who listen.

§ 2. *Flexibility.*—In true teaching, attention must first be given to that perfect flexibility of the hands upon which good playing depends, and without which, though genius itself be possessed by the player, and the finest of instruments be summoned to respond to the touch, nothing beautiful can result. An ingenious French mechanic once constructed a machine to play upon the Piano Forte. It would execute octaves, trills, and all complicated passages with the greatest precision, clearness and rapidity, in a manner which would have been very wonderful if performed by two, or even four living hands. But the tones it produced lacked life and elasticity; its touch was merely mechanical,—could be instantly recognized by the ear, and soon became positively disagreeable. Beginners are very likely so to contract and stiffen the muscles of their hands and arms as to convert these members which were designed to be flexible, into solid and firm levers which strike the keys with all the disadvantage of the wooden fingers of the automaton. They thus not only ruin their touch, but greatly increase the difficulties of playing; for, although some habitually stiff hands have, by untiring practice, attained great execution, it has been only by the severest labor, and in spite of this gigantic obstacle. As a child, who, in learning to write, grasps the pen with iron firmness, and knows not that his own strength thus employed is his greatest impediment, so such players are often entirely unconscious of any stiffness; and if informed of it, are not able to correct it immediately. Yet it depends upon the will, and can be avoided or overcome, if true flexibility is fully understood.

The first and most important point, then, in good teaching is to be sure that the pupil allows all the muscles of the hands and arms to be *entirely free from nervous rigidity and stiffness*, and to remain in a perfectly supple and easy state, such as they are in when unoccupied, and when the mind is unconscious of their existence. To train the hands of a pupil so perfectly that, while they gradually acquire that strength which is indispensible, they also retain their flexibility, requires of the teacher not only thorough knowledge, the closest attention and care, but also GREAT EXPERIENCE. The common impression that it is not important how or with whom a pupil commences, is totally erroneous. Persons who are not familiar with the modern facilities for learning the Pianist's art, have little conception how much time and labor are saved to those who are so fortunate as to employ, *from the first*, really competent and faithful teachers.

§ 3. *A really good Instrument,*—which will stand in tune well, whose tone is pure, clear and firm, and whose action is neither so easy as to render practice almost useless, nor yet so hard and heavy as to require an undue effort from the fingers, is an indispensable requisite for the best success of the pupil in *all* stages of progress. To give a beginner an inferior instrument, under the false impression that "it will answer just to learn upon," or to neglect to employ frequently a skillful tuner, even for the best of Pianos, is a mistaken economy. The beginner needs all the interest which the immediate production of fine tones can add to the charms of novelty, to counterbalance the undeniable dullness of the essential exercises. The false tones which arise from a Piano that is out of tune are positively injurious to the ear.

EXERCISES, RECREATIONS, AND PIECES.

§ 4. *Position at the Piano Forte.*—The player should sit opposite the centre of the key-board, at such a distance from it that the hands may pass freely throughout its whole length, and at such height that the elbows may be somewhat above the level of the keys.

§ 5. *The Hands* should be flat upon the top, the knuckles neither depressed nor elevated.

§ 6. *The Wrists* should be held, without stiffness, a little higher than the second joint of the middle finger.

§ 7. *The Fingers should be spread* apart so as to cover five keys, and should stand in a nearly semi-circular row, as shown in Figure 1.

Figure 1.
View of the Hands upon White Keys, as seen from above.

§ 8. *Curved position of the Fingers.*—The fingers should be curved, as shown in Figure 2. The precise curve to be employed is very important; for when they are curved too much the nails may be heard upon the keys, and freedom of action is impeded; on the other hand, when too straight, they are not easily controlled, and their power is insufficient.

Figure 2.
The Curved Position.

A common fault—bending the first joint backward—is shown in Figure 3. This should be wholly avoided. A constant effort to curve the fingers, as in Figures 2 and 4, will impart strength.*

* One of the best means of overcoming this weakness is the practice of the *Staccato* touch, described in § 36, p. 40. It is, however, well to learn the *Legato* style thoroughly before attempting the *Staccato*.

Figure 3.
The First Joint bent back. A bad position.

§ 9. *The Thumbs,* which are very liable at first to hang off the key-board, should be kept to their places, about half an inch upon the keys.

§ 10. *The Motion of the Fingers* should be vertical, and be made from the knuckle joints. The first and second joints should be slightly drawn in, as they rise, to retain nearly the same relative positions, while the fingers are elevated, that they have while they are upon the keys. Sliding the fingers upon the keys is generally objectionable.

Figure 4.
The Fourth Finger raised.

§ 11. *The particular Place upon each Key,* where the finger should strike, is shown by the rings in Figure 5, which is *drawn full size,* that the fingers of the pupil may be placed upon the paper.

Figure 5.
Rings in the Centre of the Keys show where each Finger should strike.

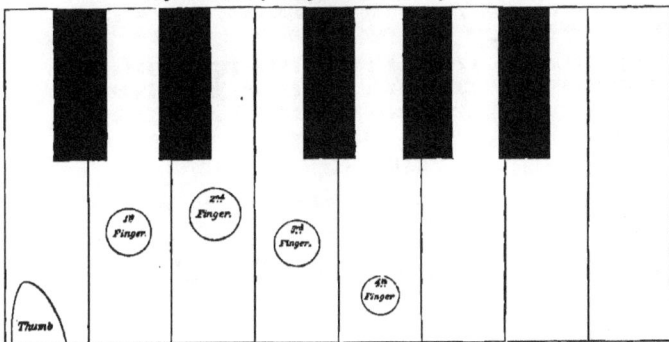

EXERCISE No. 1.

Directions to the Pupil.—Place the right hand over the five white keys, shown in Figure 5, and copy exactly the curve of the fingers, and the whole position of the hand, as exhibited in the foregoing illustrations. Everything depends upon *care* in placing, holding, and using the hand and fingers, in the beginning of practice. When the hand is brought perfectly into position, strike with the thumb several times, in the easiest possible manner; and persevere till it can move independently, without any motion of the wrist, arm, or body of the hand. This *can* be done, if it is commenced *slowly*. Train all the fingers of the Right hand, and then the Left, until some progress has been made. Do not expect to produce a powerful tone at present. To do so will certainly stiffen the hand.

Here begin to cultivate SELF CRITICISM. It is a most important element in the success of every really good musician. Without it nothing worthy can be accomplished.

§ 12. In the commencement of practice, exercises, in which the fingers to be used are indicated by figures rather than by the usual musical characters, should be employed; for the pupil can already read such exercises, and give undivided attention to training the hand. It is *indispensable* that the attention be thus undivided, for the task is a difficult one, and requires the greatest care and watchfulness by both teacher and pupil. If the latter undertakes to learn musical notation before gaining a certain degree of control of the hands and fingers, *the touch* will probably be neglected.

§ 13. *The Legato.*—The tones of the Piano Forte are produced by wires, which are made to vibrate by hammers, and to cease vibrating by dampers, both of which are moved by the finger keys. While a key is held down, the vibration of its wires is unchecked; when it rises, a damper falls upon the wires, and at once stops their sound. The word legato is used to describe that style of playing in which vibration is unceasing as tones follow each other. Each key is held fully down, that its tone may continue to sound until the precise instant when the next tone begins. If it were held longer, the tones would be heard together; if not so long, a period of silence would occur between them. The legato style of playing is employed more or less in every composition for the Piano Forte, and a complete mastery of it is indispensable to a truly correct and elegant performance even of simple music. It is indicated by a curved line called a SLUR, or LEGATO MARK, and by the word *Legato.*

§ 14. *The American Fingering.*—The following exercise is written with figures in accordance with the American system of fingering. This mark, ✕ or ✛ indicates the thumb; 1, 2, 3 and 4 the fingers, counting from the thumb.

EXERCISE No. 2.

Directions.—Practice very slowly with each hand alternately, and be very particular in watching the fingers as they rise and fall, and in *listening* to every tone, until a habit of playing in a *legato style* has been thoroughly acquired.

```
✕1✕1✕1✕1 ✕.    12121212 1.    23232323 2.    34343434 3.
✕2✕2✕2✕2 ✕.    13131313 1.    24242424 2.    ✕3✕3✕3✕3 ✕.
14141414 1.    ✕4✕4✕4✕4 ✕.   ✕1234321 ✕.    ✕2132413 2.
```

EXERCISE No. 3.

Directions.—Continue to use the hands separately, and to play very *legato*. The only way to accomplish all that is desirable, is to persevere in the most patient and careful training of the fingers, with a very slow motion. They should also move as easily as the eyelids move in winking. Raise them high before striking the keys, and curve them correctly without fail. Take particular care of the third and fourth; for, as they are weaker than the first and second fingers, they have greater need of the advantages afforded by the very best positions. Do not be impatient or weary, but do the duty of the present moment, which is, to train the hands for the production of fine effects upon the Piano Forte.

Right Hand,	4342,	4324,	3231,	3213,	212✕,	21✕2,	321✕, 1.
Left Hand,	3213,	2324,	✕12✕,	1213,	4324,	3213,	✕123, 4.
Right,	21✕1,	212✕,	3212,	3231,	4323,	4342,	3212, 1.
Left,	1213,	1213,	2343,	2342,	✕123,	1234,	2343, 4.
Right,	42✕2,	43f3,	432✕,	1,	232✕,	3431,	✕121, ✕.
Left,	31✕2,	✕213,	4321,	✕,	1234,	✕123,	✕232, 4.

§ 15. *Names of the White Keys.*—Tones are named from letters, and the keys of the instrument receive the same names as the tones which they produce. A glance at the key-board will show the pupil that the keys are of two kinds, and that the black or short keys are arranged in groups of two or three each. Each white key which is at the left of a group of two black keys, is called C; that which is at the right of the same group, is E. A little study of the letters, in Figure 6, with the practice of Exercise No. 4, will fix them in the memory. (See § 127, p. 227.)

Figure 6.
The Names of the White Keys.

EXERCISE No. 4.

Directions.—Place the Right hand over the keys of the small twice-marked octave c d e f g, and strike successively, in the order indicated by the letters, c d e f g, c d e f g, f g f d e, d f e c d, c d e f g, d e f g, d f e d e, g f e d c. Place the Left hand over the keys marked a b c d e, and strike successively, in the order indicated by the following letters, a b c d e, a b c d e, d b d b e, d b d b c, b c b a b, c d c b c, d e d c d, e d c b a.

§ 16. *Measurement of Time by Counting.*—The pupil should now be thoroughly instructed in the division of time into equal portions, called measures and parts of measures. The teacher may, perhaps, count regularly, with moderate quickness, observing the accents as marked, and always giving the falling inflection to the word "two," thus :

Óne, twò ; óne, twò ; óne, twò ; óne, twò.

When the pupil has become practically familiar with this, and can count readily, measures and parts of measures may be defined as in § 104. The teacher may then illustrate by playing the following exercise while the pupil counts: may state that bars are used as the boundaries of written measures ; that each black note, called a quarter note, represents the length of time occupied by one count ; that each rest, called a quarter rest, represents the same length of time passed in silence ; and that each open note, called a half note, represents the length of time occupied by two counts. (See Rhythmics, Chap. II and III, Theor. Dep, p. 225.)

EXERCISE No. 5.

Directions.—Count aloud with great regularity, and let the counting guide the playing. Some pupils think *they* can not count. Others think *they* can keep time without counting. Both of these common notions are false. To count well is troublesome, at first, but INDISPENSABLE. Correct counting diminishes the difficulties of execution more than any other single thing whatever. Place the Right hand over the keys c, d, e, f, g, and strike successively as the figures indicate.

Place the Left hand over the keys c, d, e, f, g, and play as follows :

§ 17. *The Staff.*—The sign of pitch; notes in connection with the staff; the former indicating the order of the succession of tones, and the latter the pitch of tones. (See Melodics, Chap. IV, Theor. Dep, p. 226.)

EXERCISE No. 6.

Directions.—Place the Right hand over the keys g, a, b, c, d, and the Left over the keys b, c, d, e, f. Keep the body of each hand perfectly unmoved throughout the whole exercise. Try to remember the absolute pitch of each tone, identifying it with its place upon the staff and its name.

ABSOLUTE PITCH, AND RELATIVE, OR SCALE PITCH REPRESENTED.   G CLEF; MODEL SCALE.

Pitch Names.   C, D, E, F, G, A, B, C, B, A, G, F, E, D, C, B, C, D, F, E, C, D, F, E, C, D, B, G, A, D, C, B, C.

Scale Names.   I, II, III, IV, V, VI, VII, VIII, VII, VI, V, IV, III, II, I, VII, I, II, IV, III, I, II, VII, V, VI, II, VIII, VII, VIII.
(1)   (2)

In the use of the staff, the pupil will be assisted by observing that the interval of a second (§ 133, p. 228.) is indicated by contiguous degrees, as from a line to the space above it, or from a space to the line above it. The interval of a third skips one degree, from line to line, or from space to space. (See Chap. VII, Theor. Dep, p. 228.) Roman numerals are used throughout the work to indicate scale relationship.

FIRST RECREATION.

Directions.—Place the Right hand upon the keys g, a, b, c, d, and the Left upon c, d, e, f, g. Both thumbs cover the same key, but do not play at the same time; the one not in use may turn under the first finger. The body of each hand should remain unmoved throughout the piece. COUNT.

G F E D C D E   G A B C D C B

SECOND RECREATION.

Directions.—Place the Right hand over the keys c, d, e, f, g, and the Left over b, c, d, e, f. After playing eight measures, lift the Right hand, *without deranging the fingers,* and place it over the keys g, a, b, c, d. COUNT ALOUD, *One, Two, Three,* in each measure.

(1) This B is VII of a scale below I.   (2) This D is II of a scale above VIII. (See § 126, p. 227.)

TRIPLE MEASURE.   DOTTED HALF NOTE.   WHOLE REST.

[musical notation — Right hand: C D E G F D C]

[musical notation — Left hand: C B C E D C B]

[musical notation — G A B]

TABULAR VIEW OF DIFFERENT FORMS IN DOUBLE MEASURE.

Primitive.....................

Derivative........................

TABULAR VIEW OF DIFFERENT FORMS IN TRIPLE MEASURE.

Primitive Form...................

First Derivative ....

Second Derivative ....

§ 18. *The Hand relatively the same on every part of the Key-board.*— Whenever the keys to be struck are so far to the right or left that the arm forms an angle with them, the wrist should turn to allow the fingers and hand to retain precisely the same relation to the keys that they have when the arm is straight. This is illustrated by Figure 7, which shows the Right hand in a position to play c, d, e, f, g; by Figure 8, which shows the same hand over c, d, e, f, g; and by Figure 9, which shows the hand over c, d, e, f, g. In all these positions the fingers rise and fall in the same vertical planes as the keys upon which they play. The lines (A, B,) in the cuts represent these planes, being parallel to the sides of both fingers and keys.

Figure 7.   *Figure 8.*   *Figure 9.*

EXERCISE No. 7.

Directions.—Place the Right hand over the keys g, a, b, c, d, and the Left over g, a, b, c, d. Turn the Left wrist, that the fingers may move in the same planes as the keys. Count aloud, ONE, TWO, THREE, FOUR, in each measure.

QUADRUPLE MEASURE.   PRIMITIVE FORM.   HALF REST.

G A B C D C B A G

THIRD RECREATION.

Directions.—Avoid deranging the fingers in changing the position of the hand. Move the whole hand at once.

B C B A G A

TABULAR VIEW OF DIFFERENT FORMS IN QUADRUPLE MEASURE.*

Primitive, or most simple form......

First Derivative.......................

Second Derivative.....................

Third Derivative.......................

* It is important that the teacher should impart to the pupil a clear idea of rhythmic formations. The latter can then, by considering the primitive form in every case, analyze and quickly comprehend any derived form that may occur. A comparison of the relative length of notes with the value of money has been found to assist many pupils. If the whole note (○) is considered to represent a dollar, the half note (♩) will represent fifty cents, the quarter note (♩) twenty-five cents, the (♪) twelve and a half cents, the (♪') thirty-seven and a half cents, &c.

EXERCISE No. 8.

Directions.—To play the thirteenth measure, place the hand upon g, a, b, c, d. In the twenty-ninth, the Right thumb is upon c. In the thirty-seventh, it is upon g. Particular care should be exercised in placing the hand in this last position, as in

Figure 10.

This exercise affords good practice in turning the wrists. The fingers should be kept in their relative positions while the hand is moved from one place to another, and a habit of fitting them instantly to the keys to be played should be formed. Such a habit will save hours of practice, and assist greatly in playing at sight.

FOURTH RECREATION.

BEYER.

At this stage of progress the learner should commence the practice of the ACCENT EXERCISES with No. 56, p. 147. They should be interspersed with all the Recreations, Pieces, and other Exercises, that follow.

FIFTH RECREATION.

BEYER.

§ 19. ***Absolute Pitch. G Clef.***—The pupil should now learn thoroughly the absolute pitch of all the tones indicated by the G Clef. Lines and spaces should be learned separately. To repeat aloud, several times daily, the name of each tone, describing the degree of the staff which indicates it, and striking simultaneously the key which produces it, is a good mode of fixing it in the memory.

Figure 11.

LINES OF TREBLE STAFF.

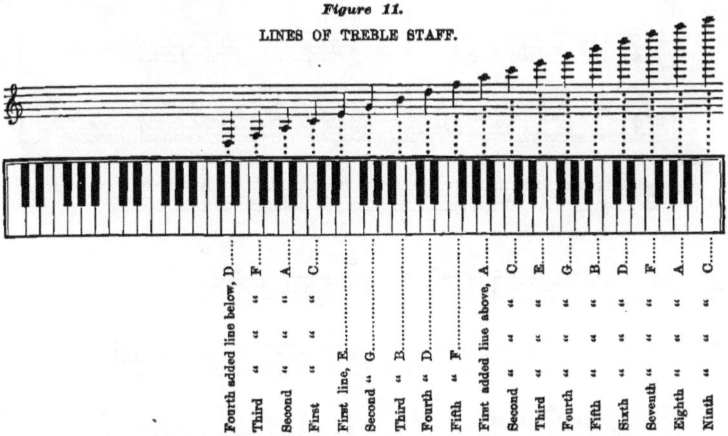

§ 20. ***The Repeat.***—Dots, placed before a bar, thus: (:|) indicate repetition of the preceding strain. Dots after a bar, thus: (|:) indicate repetition of the following strain.

§ 21. ***The Tie.***—Two notes, representing the same pitch, are sometimes united so as to indicate one tone only, with a length equal to that of both notes. They are marked with a curved line, called a TIE, over or under them, thus:

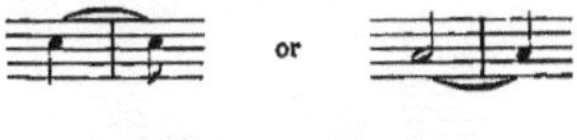

SIXTH RECREATION.

BEYER

SEVENTH RECREATION.

BEYER.

EIGHTH RECREATION.

Directions.—Place the Left hand over c, d, e, f, g.   Count four in each measure.

F CLEF.   EIGHTH NOTES.

BERTINI.

§ 22. *The Chromatic Scale.*—(§ 140, p. 228, § 189, p. 234.) All the black keys are played by the second finger; the hand being brought into such a position in relation to each, that the finger may rise and fall in the same vertical plane with the key.   The change from one position to another is made only *while the thumb is playing.*   The thumb turns under to take its key, while the second finger plays, but without causing any movement of the body of the hand.   The curve of the second finger should be as great upon the black keys as upon the white.   (See § 8, p. 6, and Fig. 14, p. 27.)

(1) This scale, which requires the thumb to turn under the hand more frequently, but a less distance, than the Diatonic scales, should therefore precede them.   It may be taught very easily by use of the key-board alone.   Names of tones and modes of writing them should be taught after the playing has become familiar.

EXERCISE No. 9.

Directions.—Practice this scale *daily* many times; at first, ascending with the Right hand, and descending with the Left, separately, very slowly, and with unabated care as to every motion. After some facility has been acquired, play both ways with each hand, one at a time; as skill in execution increases, play more and more rapidly, without, however, accelerating the time in any one trial. (See §§ 141, 142 and 143, p. 228.)

RIGHT HAND.   **LEFT HAND.**

RIGHT.   **LEFT.**

§ 23. *Absolute Pitch. F Clef.*—The pupil should now learn thoroughly the absolute pitch of all the tones indicated by the F Clef. The mode of doing this should be similar to that recommended for the G Clef.

Figure 12.

LINES UPON THE BASE STAFF.

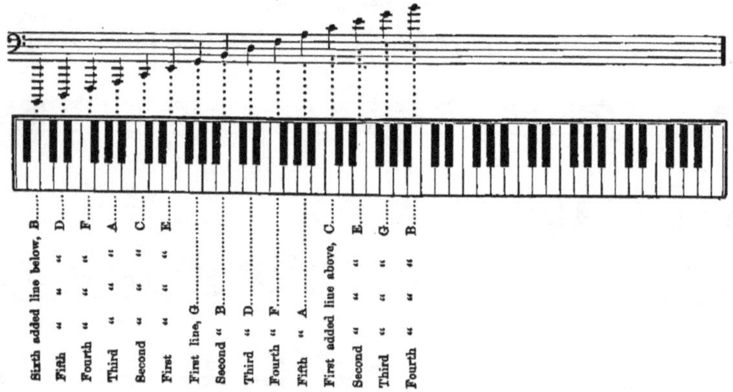

NINTH RECREATION.

BEYER.

Legato.

§ 24. Use of the Hand in Diatonic Scales.—The hand takes two positions in each octave, remaining in the first until the thumb, having turned under the fingers, has struck the first key of the second position, then the hand and the arm, while supported by the thumb, are instantly changed to that position. The fingers are spread over their proper keys precisely as in five-finger exercises, and retain their relative positions perfectly while the hand, as a whole, is moved. The wrist, wherever the arm is at an angle with the keys, turns to allow the fingers equal opportunity in all positions to move in nearly the same vertical planes as the keys. (See § 18, p. 11.) A slight turning of the hand inward lessens the distance to be reached by the thumb, and therefore diminishes the difficulty. The importance of attaining perfection in the manner of changing the position of the hand can hardly be over-estimated; the clearness, equality, rapidity and beauty of running passages being greatly dependent upon this change. In rapid playing, by a well trained hand, the changes become almost imperceptible, and the hand appears to be constantly moving sidewise. Figure 13 shows the position of the hand in four octaves of the scale of C. The fourth finger is used only upon the last note, and the third only once in each octave, yet these are always held over their proper keys, ready for use.

Figure 13.

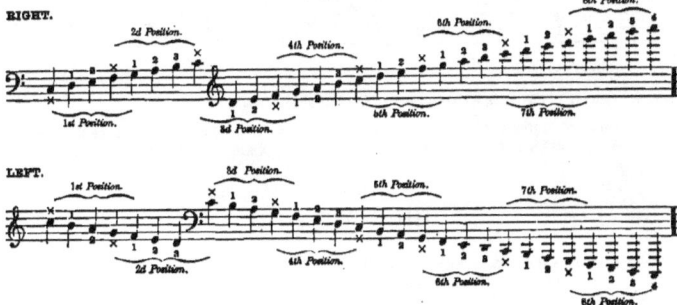

EXERCISE No. 10.

Directions.—Place the Right hand several times in each of the eight positions of Figure 13, to practice turning the wrist. Take the fifth position, and repeatedly pass the thumb from C to F, without rolling the arm or moving the body of the hand. Very small hands may be unable to reach the thumb-key without a slight movement; but those of ordinary size can do it easily. Take the sixth position, and pass the thumb from F to C, turning the hand slightly around while upon the tip of the third finger, to reach C, but without in the least rolling the arm. In descending, move the whole hand and arm together, while the thumb bends under to retain its key until all the fingers have reached their new places; otherwise the legato can not be preserved. Then go up and down several times through the eight positions, striking only the keys to be taken by the thumb and third finger, and perfecting the changes. Thus prepared, play every tone through four octaves, *a little slower than one sound in a second of time.* Keep the hand flat upon the top. Make all the tones equal in power, in length, and perfectly legato. Practice thus every day many times. Train the Left hand in a similar manner, even more than the right.

TENTH RECREATION.

Direction. — Curve the third finger well upon the B♭.

BEYER.

To assist the memory of the pupil, a classification of the scales is important.

§ 25. *First Class of Major Scales.*[1]—The third finger of the Right hand upon VII, and the third finger of the Left upon II. (§ 155, p. 229, and § 189, 2, p. 234.) The scales of C, G, D, A, and E belong to this class.

EXERCISE No. 11.

Directions. — Practice these scales with each hand separately, and remember that those who would learn them quickly must, at first, play no faster than at the rate of one sound per second. Criticise every movement, and NEVER MAKE A MISTAKE. It is not difficult to destroy the value of correct practice. Though some commendable effort may be made, yet, if an equal amount of careless, inaccurate work be done, no real progress can result. TWENTY-FIVE ABSOLUTELY CORRECT REPETITIONS of any scale will generally overcome its difficulty. Then it can

(1) The best way, perhaps, to teach the scales is to request the pupil to select the component tones of each scale in the first class, in accordance with the formula, (See § 155,) and to write the letters which represent them, and figures for the fingering, thus:

	I.	II.	III.	IV.	V.	VI.	VII.	VIII.
	C,	D,	E,	F,	G,	A,	B,	C.
	G,	A,	B,	C,	D,	E,	F♯,	G.
	D,	E,	F♯,	G,	A,	B,	C♯,	D.
	A,	B,	C♯,	D,	E,	F♯,	G♯,	A.
	E,	F♯,	G♯,	A,	B,	C♯,	D♯,	E.
Right,	×,	1,	2,	×,	1,	2,	3,	×.
Left,	×,	3,	2,	1,	×,	3,	2,	1, ×.

The pupil can then play them all without any use of notes, can give undivided attention to the hands, and can, in a short time, remember both scales and fingering perfectly. The other classes may then follow.

gradually be played more and more rapidly until the highest speed is attained.   Depend, as soon as possible, entirely upon the memory.

8va . . . ., an abbreviation of the Italian word *Ottava*, octave, indicates that tones should be played an octave higher or lower than the true pitch of the notes, as it is placed over or under them.   It continues in force only to the end of the waived or dotted line, but to make it certain that the pitch is restored, the word *Loco*, in the place, is frequently written after it.

MAJOR SCALES.

SCALE OF C.   COMPONENT TONES, C, D, E, F, G, A, B.

SCALE OF G.   COMPONENT TONES, G, A, B, C, D, E, F♯.

SCALE OF D.   Component Tones, D, E, F♯, G, A, B, C♯.

SCALE OF A.   Component Tones, A, B, C♯, D, E, F♯, G♯.

SCALE OF E.   Component Tones, E, F♯, G♯, A, B, C♯, D♯.

§ 26. *The Slur as a Mark of Expression.*—When the slur is placed over two notes, indicating different pitch, thus: or a group of notes, thus: it signifies not only *legato* (§ 13, p. 8), but also that the first tone is accented, and that the second, or the last of the group, is unaccented and somewhat staccato. (See § 36, p. 40.)

ELEVENTH RECREATION.

Directions.—Count eight in each measure. Lift the fingers entirely off from the keys at the rests, and give each rest its full length.

KEY OF A. EIGHTH RESTS. SLURS.

§ 27. *How Artists Play at Sight.*—The great secret of playing at sight is the ABILITY TO ANALYZE MUSIC. The accomplished Pianist instantly recognizes each passage as one of a *class of passages* with which he is familiar. He therefore knows what position of the hand and what fingers must be chosen; seizes upon the divisions and subdivisions of measures in regard to time; notices what chords and what tones are to be particularly emphatic; and thus, triumphing over the mechanical difficulties, and making available all his knowledge and skill previously acquired, is able to form some conception of the internal meaning of a musical composition, and so to interpret it more or less perfectly.

Analysis has been greatly neglected in the study of music; yet its principles are very simple, and a slight attention to it gives gratifying results. (See Chapters XVI and XVII, Theoretical Department, p. 234.)

TWELFTH RECREATION.

§ 28. *Analysis of the Fingering.*—A very slight examination of the Base in this Recreation will show the pupil that it is a simple five-finger passage, E̱, F♯, G♯, A̱, Ḇ, (See § 187, p. 234.) The Treble is not so clear; but that also is nothing more than two such passages combined. The first position for the Right hand is Ḇ, C♯, D♯, E̱, F♯, and the third finger strikes the first note.[1] While the second finger is playing the fifth note, the thumb turns under to E, which is the first note of the second position E̱, F♯, G♯, A̱, Ḇ. While the thumb holds the tenth note the hand changes back again to the first position, and is prepared for all that follows.

The notes are purposely left without figures, that the pupil may learn to think upon the subject. The study of analysis will teach when and where to change the position of the hand, and how to select the fingers.

BERTINI.

§ 29. *Scales for both Hands, Contrary Motion.*—The pupil who has diligently practiced the scales as they have thus far been given, is now prepared to use the hands together. Contrary motion, requiring the hands to move towards, or from each other, is less difficult at first, in this class of scales, than parallel motion, in which they move up or down together.

EXERCISE No. 12.

Directions.—If the fingering of these scales is not yet perfectly familiar, commit it to memory with no delay. It is as indispensable for music as is spelling for writing a language. (See §§ 22, p. 17, and 25, p. 20.)

[1] The word *note* is here employed to signify the *tone* indicated by the note. This use of it, though not strictly correct, is very common, and avoids circumlocution.

THIRTEENTH RECREATION.

§ 30. *Analysis of the Fingering.*—The first three, and the last four measures consist of the scale of A, in contrary motion. The fourth measure in the Right-hand part is marked 1, exceptionally, instead of 3, because the hand ascends immediately. In the fourth, fifth and sixth measures the scale continues in the Left-hand part. The seventh to the nineteenth measures inclusive, are five-finger passages. Each change of position is indicated by a single finger mark. The twentieth measure in the Left hand part is exceptional.[1]

BERTINI. *Arr.*

EXERCISE No. 13.

To be Fingered by the Pupil. — All the passages marked thus, ⌐⌐⌐ are parts of the scale of C, and are fingered accordingly. All marked thus, ⌐⌐⌐ are five-finger passages C—G. The first finger is used exceptionally in the twelfth and fourteenth measures.

BEYER.

(1) The teacher should see that the pupil clearly understands the *principles* which apply in fingering this piece; and although more practical advantage will be gained by playing it correctly, without further marking, yet, if it is found necessary to insure accuracy, all the notes should be marked.

§ 31. *Curve of the Fingers upon Black Keys.* —In playing black keys, learners are very liable to straighten the fingers. They should curve them as fully as upon white keys. Figure 14, which is drawn full size, that the hand of the pupil may be placed upon the paper, indicates the points that should be touched by fingers and thumb of the Right hand, in playing the scale of B. A comparison of this with Figure 5, shows that the hand is further upon the key-board in playing black keys than white.

Figure 14.

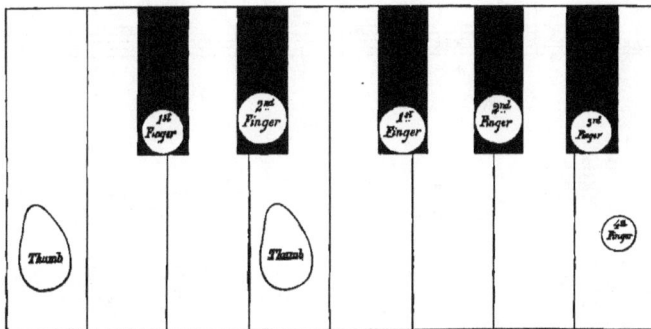

§ 32. *The Second Class of Major Scales.*—Each of the three scales forming the second class employs *all the black keys and two white ones* in every octave. The latter are played by the thumb, and the former by the fingers in groups; the two black keys thus: { Right. $C\sharp$, $D\sharp$, and the three thus: { Right. $F\sharp$, $G\sharp$, $A\sharp$. { Left. 2 1 { Left. 3 2 1

The scales of B, $F\sharp$ and $C\sharp$ belong to this class. They are written with either sharps or flats, according to the fancy of composers. It is therefore necessary for the pupil's eye to be familiar with them in both forms.

EXERCISE No. 14.

Directions.—Take care to remember the white keys in each scale.   Parallel motion, in this class, is easier than
contrary, when the hands are first brought together.

MAJOR SCALES.

SCALE OF B, or C♭.   Component Tones,   { B, C♯, D♯, E, F♯, G♯, A♯.
                                           { C♭, D♭, E♭, F♭, G♭, A♭, B♭.

SCALE OF F♯ or G♭. Component Tones, $\begin{cases} \text{F♯, G♯, A♯, B, C♯, D♯, E♯.} \\ \text{G♭, A♭, B♭, C♭, D♭, E♭, F.} \end{cases}$

SCALE OF C♯, or D♭.   COMPONENT TONES, { C♯, D♯, E♯, F♯, G♯, A♯, B♯. / D♭, E♭, F, G♭, A♭, B♭, C.

FOURTEENTH RECREATION.

Directions.—Practice this, and the four following Recreations, with care. They will facilitate the reading of many modern compositions which are written in these keys, will render all simple keys less difficult, and will aid in acquiring the important habit of constantly keeping in mind the signature while playing. Be careful to curve the fingers correctly upon the black keys. (See directions and cut.-Fig. 40. page 156.)

BEYER.

FIFTEENTH RECREATION.

BEYER.

SIXTEENTH RECREATION.

BEYER.

SEVENTEENTH RECREATION.

BEYER.

EIGHTEENTH RECREATION.

BEYER.

§ 33. *The Third Class of Major Scales.*—The four scales belonging to this class are invariably written with flats. They are F, B♭, E♭ and A♭. Their fingering is perfectly uniform in the Right hand, the third finger being always placed upon B♭. In the scale of F the third finger of the Left hand is placed upon G, and in the scales of B♭, E♭, and A♭ upon IV.

EXERCISE No. 15.

MAJOR SCALES.

SCALE OF F.   COMPONENT TONES, F, G, A, B♭, C, D, E.

SCALE OF B♭.   Component Tones, B♭, C, D, E♭, F, G, A.

SCALE OF E♭.   Component Tones, E♭, F, G, A♭, B♭, C, D.

SCALE OF A♭.   Component Tones, A♭, B♭, C, D♭, E♭, F, G.

NINETEENTH RECREATION.

BEYER.

§ 34. *Appoggiaturas.*—The small notes, in the following Recreation, should be unaccented, and played very lightly and quickly, as if written thus:

They are called APPOGGIATURAS. (See §§ 77, p. 131, and 162, p. 230.)

TWENTIETH RECREATION.

BEYER.

TWENTY-FIRST RECREATION.

Directions.—Analyze this, and the next two pieces, in accordance with the foregoing principles. Mark the fingering, and submit it to the teacher for correction. In order to know what finger commences any passage of the First Class, compare its highest and lowest notes, and thus ascertain the place of the hand. (See §§ 187 and 188, p. 234.) For passages of the Second Class follow the fingering of the Scales in the same keys. (See § 189, p. 234.)

BEYER.

TWENTY-SECOND RECREATION.

KNORR.

TWENTY-THIRD RECREATION.

§ 35. *Extended Positions.*—Hitherto the fingers have, in no single instance, been required to play any other keys than those directly under them : this was highly important for the best training of the hand ; but now, as the field becomes wider, they must learn to extend and contract, and adapt themselves readily to a great variety of positions. And here the first general rule should receive special attention. (§ 183, p. 234.) If scrupulously observed, it will save both time and labor.

EXERCISE No. 16.

Directions. — Give particular attention to fitting the fingers instantly to six, seven or eight keys, as the positions require : play with the body of the hand perfectly quiet. Make the change while upon the last note in each position.

TWENTY-FOURTH RECREATION.

EXTENDED POSITIONS IN THE RIGHT HAND.   TRIPLETS.   (See § 103, p. 225.)

BEYER.

EXERCISE No. 17.

REVIEW OF THE MAJOR SCALES.   SIXTEENTH NOTES.

Directions.—The pupil has now learned the construction and fingering of all the Major Scales, and should practice them every day from memory, in both parallel and contrary motion. Give five minutes of continuous labor daily to each key, and these scales will soon become very familiar. Commence at the rate of one hundred sounds in a minute: then gradually increase the speed to its utmost limit, and continue some time at that rate. Finally, when the hands are weary, end the practicing by playing as slowly as at first.

THE ACCENT EXERCISES UPON CHROMATIC AND DIATONIC SCALES should now be commenced with Nos. 106 and 118, and continued in connection with all the pieces that follow, at the discretion of the teacher.

§ 36. *The Staccato Touch.*—That style of playing which allows the dampers to fall upon the wires, and stop their vibration instantly after each tone is heard, is called STACCATO. (See § 13, p. 8.) The most elastic touch, for the staccato style, by which clear and brilliant tones are produced without impeding the freest action of the dampers, is attained in the following manner : The finger is partly straightened over the key to be struck, as shown in Fig. 15. Then the first and second joints are suddenly bent into the position shown in Fig. 16. While they are bending, the key is touched just enough to produce the desired effect. The thumb produces the same effect by sliding off the end of the key.

Figure 15.	**Figure 16.**

This mode of practicing staccato passages is very useful in giving strength to the first and the second joints of the fingers, and thus improving the hand. Staccato is indicated by dots or points over or under notes, thus :

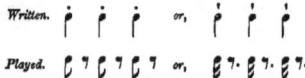

EXERCISE No. 18.

THIRTY-SECOND NOTES.

Directions.— In the following exercise, the legato and staccato styles are alternated. Be sure either to perfectly connect, or clearly detach the tones, as the marking directs. In order to derive the greatest benefit from preliminary slow practice, the finger should be straightened more than in Fig. 15, and the motion made more sweeping than in the rapid execution of a well-trained hand. Strike with each finger in the manner above described, and instantly bend it up for every staccato, as though the key were too hot to be held. Do not raise the hand.

EXERCISE No. 19.

Directions.—The object of this exercise is to aid in acquiring celerity. Placing the finger firmly upon the first key of each passage, and looking over the other keys to be struck—thinking what is to be done—taking aim, so to speak—the small notes are played with ALL POSSIBLE IMPETUOSITY, imitating the roll of a drum. Great care is necessary, in counting strictly, in sustaining the long tones as nearly as possible their entire length, and in striking promptly with the staccato touch the last tone in each passage. Every measure should be repeated many times in immediate succession until the hands are weary : then let them rest. When sufficient celerity of execution has been acquired, the whole exercise should be played in strict time, from beginning to end without interruption. Then, as skill increases, without acceleration in any one trial, the whole movement should be more and more rapid.

TWENTY-FIFTH RECREATION.

Directions.—Examine carefully the fingering of the passages, that the extended positions may be fully understood. The first Right-hand position is over six keys, G̈ B C D E. The second is over seven keys, G̈ C♯ D E F.

§ 37. The Hand moved by Extension. — Exercise No. 20 shows some of the many ways in which the hand may be moved by combining different positions. In the first measure the hand takes a position which includes six keys ascending, and five descending, thus: C E F G A G F E D. The next six measures are constructed upon the model of the first. The ninth measure has a six-key position descending, and a five-key ascending. It also serves as a model for several measures. The pupil can, in like manner, carry out each of the remaining measures. It will be a very useful exercise if practiced thoroughly. The Left hand is to play an octave lower than the Right, reading from the same notes.

EXERCISE No. 20.

§ 38. *Minute counting.* — Accuracy in keeping time, and the power of judging of the length of tones, is much sooner acquired by those who practice counting minute divisions of measures, than by others. The following measures, for example, require much less skill, when counted as the figures above the notes indicate, than when counted in the manner shown below them.

Figure 17.

Inserting the word "*and*" between countings is, to say the least, only partly efficacious, and not as truly scientific as minute counting. It is a very useful exercise for the pupil to strike with a pencil, upon any hard surface, dividing parts of measures accurately, thus:

Figure 18.

§ 39. *Practical Transposition.* — It often happens that performers wish to change the place of a musical composition, taking it higher or lower than they find it written. Such changing, without destroying the identity of scale-relationship, is called TRANSPOSING from one key to another. The ability to transpose with ease the ordinary accompaniments of vocal music is a very important one for the pupil.

TWENTY-SIXTH RECREATION.

Directions. — Write this piece in the key of G, and practice it in both C and G. A comparison of the two scales, thus :—

	I.	II.	III. IV.	V.	VI.	VII. VIII.
	C	D	E F	G	A	B C
	G	A	B C	D	E	F♯ G

will show, at once, what letters to use. For I., which is C in the key written, G will be required in the transposition. For II., A will be required, &c.

Count eight in each measure. (See § 102, p. 225.)

First Measure in C.   First Measure in G.

BEYER.

§ 40. *The Hand moved by Contraction.*—An important mode of changing the position of the hand is employed in Exercise No. 21. While playing the last note before each change, the finger that is to play the next note is brought to its place, and during its use the other fingers are extended.

EXERCISE No. 21.

Directions.—Consider the first group in each measure as the germ from which a long passage grows, and in order to derive the full benefit from the exercise, carry it through at least two octaves with each mode of fingering.

§ 41. *Analysis of the Fingering.*—This piece includes a variety of positions, and will be very instructive the pupil, if studied until clearly understood. Right hand: In measures 1, 2, 3, 4, part of 5, 9, 10, 11, and 12, a seve key position, slightly varied, is used, thus: B, or C♯, E, or E♯, F♯, G♯, A; in 6, 7, 8, and the last part of 15, a fi key position, E,——B; in 13, 21, 22, 29, 31, and 32, a five-key position, B,——F♯; in 14, part of 15, 23, and 24, a si key position, B,——G♯; in 17, 18, 19, 20, 25, 26, 27, and 28, a six-key position, A, C♯, or C♮, D♯, E, F♯, or F♮. passing from 24 to 25, a contraction occurs, D♯, E, and in 30, an extension, C♯, A, and an omission of the first finger passing from F♯ to E. The Left-hand part is all simple until 29, 30, and 31, where a change is made for every measu by contraction.

Directions.—Count six in each measure. Observe the Double Sharp in the twenty-second measure. (§ 143, p. 22 The Double Sharp is here represented by ⚹, in order to distinguish it from the thumb mark. In musical compositio generally the pupil will find it written thus, ×.

TWENTY-SEVENTH RECREATION.

§ 42. *Thirds.*—In playing thirds it is difficult to strike both tones at the same instant. The only test is the ear, and it is necessary to listen closely and be sure that one tone is not heard before the other. Both tones also must be strictly legato. (See Chapter VII, Theoretical Dept, p. 228.)

EXERCISE No. 22.

FIVE-FINGER EXERCISE IN THIRDS.

Directions.—Play as slowly, and watch the fingers as closely as in the first exercises. Do not move the body of the hand, or stiffen the muscles. Repeat each measure at least twenty times before passing to the next.

Change the hands dexterously, and preserve the legato in the following.

BEYER.

TWENTY-EIGHTH RECREATION.

§ 43. *Analysis of the Measures.* — Six should be counted for each measure; one for every ♪ — The ♪ in the Treble has a count and a half, the ♪ having the last half of the second count. The ♪ has three counts. The Base and Treble go together thus: The seventh measure thus:

BEYER.

§ 44. *Repetition or Reiteration of Tones.* —It is generally very difficult for beginners to avoid stiffening the hand and raising the arm whenever tones are consecutively repeated. Such repetitions, therefore, have, thus far, been excluded. They may be performed in three ways: first, by changing the fingers; second, by continued action of the same finger; and third, by action of the wrist.

§ 45. *In repetition by changing the Fingers,* the hand is drawn back to the end of the key, and the staccato touch is used by each finger in succession. (See § 36, p. 40.) The change from one finger to another in the reverse order of their numbers, causes a movement of the Right hand upward, and of the Left downward upon the key-board. The wrist should be perfectly flexible.

EXERCISE No. 23.

TWENTY-NINTH RECREATION.

§ 46. *Repetition by continued action of the same Finger* should be made wholly from the knuckle join
the arm and hand being perfectly quiet. Practice is needed to enable beginners to perform it easily.

The following exercise, though very dry and uninteresting, is so useful, not only in training the fingers to repe
well, but also in rendering each one of them independent, that it will repay all the labor that may be bestowed upon i
The keys that are held should receive no more pressure than just enough to keep them fully down. Stiffness must b
wholly avoided.

EXERCISE No. 24.

Directions. — Place the Right hand upon the keys g, a, b, c, d, and the Left an octave lower; then, without u
of notes, exercise the fingers as follows: Hold X while striking many times with each of the fingers. Hold 1, whi
striking X, 2, 3 and 4, each many times. In like manner, hold each of the others.

Hold X and 4 while striking	1 1 1 1	2 2 2 2	3 3 3 3	&c.
" X " 3 " "	1 1 1 1	2 2 2 2	4 4 4 4	"
" X " 2 " "	1 1 1 1	3 3 3 3	4 4 4 4	"
" X " 1 " "	2 2 2 2	3 3 3 3	4 4 4 4	"
" 1 " 2 " "	X X X X	3 3 3 3	4 4 4 4	"
" 1 " 3 " "	X X X X	2 2 2 2	4 4 4 4	"
" 1 " 4 " "	3 3 3 3	2 2 2 2	X X X X	"
" 2 " 3 " "	1 1 1 1	X X X X	4 4 4 4	"
" 2 " 4 " "	3 3 3 3	1 1 1 1	X X X X	"
" 3 " 4 " "	X X X X	1 1 1 1	2 2 2 2	"

Also, play from the notes, as follows:

§ 47.—*Repetition by Action of the Wrist* is generally used where double notes or chords occur. The fingers are curved as in five-finger exercises, but are spread sufficiently to cover the keys to be played. The joints of the fingers do not move at all, but the *whole hand* rises and falls *from the wrist*, while the arm is kept perfectly still. Young pupils invariably use this motion *after* striking the keys with the arm. They should *first* raise the *hand*, and, in producing the tones, strike with it, as with a hammer.

EXERCISE No. 25.

Directions.—Train each hand separately, until some ease in using the wrist has been acquired. Make the time of the triplets clear and distinct. The Left hand is to play an octave lower than the Right, reading from the same notes.

THIRTIETH RECREATION.

Question for the Pupil: What principles, already explained, are involved in the fingering of this piece?

§ 48. *Studies. Etudes.*—A composition, designed to furnish special training for students in music, is called a STUDY, or, using the French term, an ETUDE. Though many studies are interesting, few are really attractive. They are, however, indispensable; and no pieces, composed with other objects in view, can possibly take the place of good studies. The true mode of using Studies is highly important; but merely playing them a few times, accomplishes very little. The first requisite is to learn them perfectly, with a very slow movement. When one of them can be performed thus, WITHOUT A SINGLE MISTAKE, it should be repeated a great number of times in the course of months, with unabated care, and gradually quicker and quicker, until, by such practice, the hands attain great skill and celerity in the particular manner of playing which that study is designed to develop.

§ 49. *Preparation for acquiring the Trill.*—One of the most elegant embellishments possible in music is a really beautiful Trill, which is produced by a rapid, evenly balanced alternation of two tones, at the interval of a second. Its elegance and beauty depend upon the perfection with which its tones are executed. A limping, jerking, faltering trill, with too many or too few sounds, is an outrage upon musical feeling. How then shall the pupil acquire the ability to trill elegantly? The answer must be the same it would be to a similar question concerning the Scales. Carefully poised fingers must play the trill so slowly at first that it may be done perfectly; and speed must be gradually attained.

The following excellent Study by Bertini, if rightly practiced, is an admirable preparatory exercise.

EXERCISE No. 26.

TRILL STUDY.

Directions.—Count eight in each measure, and persevere in playing no faster than sixty counts in a minute, until the whole study can be played without rolling or shaking the hand in the least; without hesitation or faltering, and without an *error.* So much gained, in a few weeks, by daily practice, the speed may be increased to one hundred and fifty counts in a minute; and such of the fingers as have been thus trained, will have acquired facility in executing the trill. A strong accent upon the first and third parts of the measures will assist in the beginning of practice.

TRILL STUDY.

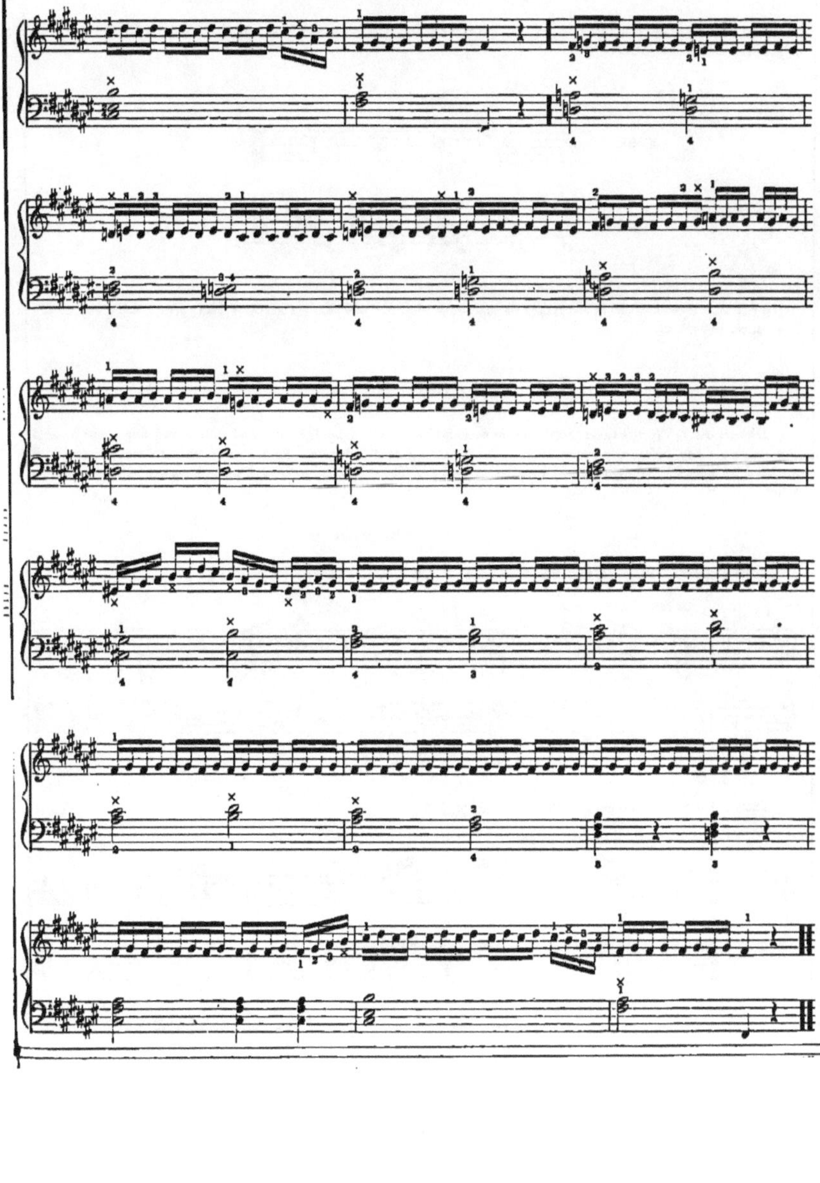

§ 50. *Sign of Abbreviation.*—To avoid the necessity of writing the same group of notes repeatedly, a sign of abbreviation is used, thus :

Figure 19.

Written :

Played : .

§ 51. *The Triad of I,* in every key, is composed of I, III and V.   (See Chap. XIV, p. 231, and § 191, p. 235 Theoretical Department.

EXERCISE No. 27.

Directions.—Practice these chords first in their broken forms, extending the hand so that each finger may be held over its proper key, before any one is struck. Do not straighten the fingers. Repeat each measure many times, until the hand becomes somewhat accustomed to the extension. These Triads may be broken in many ways, not shown below.

KEY OF C.   TRIAD OF I.

FIRST POSITION.   Fingered with the Right hand, × 1 2 4, and with the Left, × 1 3 4.

I.   *The same Chord broken.*

SECOND POSITION.   Fingered with each hand, × 1 3 4.

I.   *The same Chord broken.*

THIRD POSITION.   Fingered with the Right hand, ╳ 1 3 4, and with the Left, ╳ 1 2 4.

L   *The same Chord broken.*

THE ACCENT EXERCISES UPON BROKEN CHORDS, commencing with No. 154, p. 185, should now be gradually introduced, at the discretion of the teacher.

THIRTY-FIRST RECREATION.

Directions.—Play to the first double bar; repeat, omitting measures marked "*First time.*" After playing the second strain, repeat the first again, omitting the same measures, and close at the word *Fine.* This last repetition is indicated by the Italian words *Da Capo al Fine*, abbreviated *D. C.* In passing from the twenty-sixth measure to the first, lift the Left hand from the position G̅—D̅, and place it over C̅—G̅. No special care is needed to make any of the tones legato, but perfect flexibility in all the muscles is essential. Bring out clearly the repetitions of D in the Base. Observe the staccato marks.

26

In learning the Minor Scales, a classification, with reference to their fingering, is useful to assist the memory. (See Chap. X, p. 230 Theor. Dept. and § 189, 2, p. 234.)

§ 52. *First Class of Minor Scales.* — The scales of C, G, D, A and E, Minor, belong to this class, and have the third finger of the Right hand on VII, and the third finger of the Left on II.

EXERCISE No. 28.

MINOR SCALES.

SCALE OF C MINOR.   COMPONENT TONES, C, D, E♭, F, G, A♭ or A♮, B♮.

SCALE OF G MINOR.   COMPONENT TONES, G, A, B♭, C, D, E♭ or E♮, F♯.

SCALE OF D MINOR.   COMPONENT TONES, D, E, F, G, A, B♭ or B♮, C♯.

SCALE OF A MINOR.   COMPONENT TONES, A, B, C, D, E, F or F♯, G♯.

SCALE OF E MINOR.   Component Tones, E, F♯, G, A, B, C or C♯, D♯.

§ 53. *Second Class of Minor Scales.*—The scales of B, F♯ and C♯ Minor belong to this class, and have the third finger of the Left hand on F♯. The scales of B and C♯ Minor have the third finger of the Right hand on A or A♯. The scale of F♯ Minor has the third of the Right on D or D♯.

EXERCISE No. 29.

SCALE OF B MINOR.   Component Tones, B, C♯, D, E, F♯, G or G♯, A♯.

SCALE OF F♯ MINOR.   Component Tones, F♯, G♯, A, B, C♯, D or D♯, E♯. (1)

SCALE OF C♯ MINOR.   Component Tones, C♯, D♯, E, F♯, G♯, A or A♯, B♯.

(1) Be careful, in descending with the Right hand, to make E♯ legato; holding it firmly with the thumb while the hand turns to enable the third finger to strike D♯.

§ 54. *Third Class of Minor Scales.*—The scales of F, B♭ or A♯, E♭ or D♯, and A♭ or G♯ minor, belong to this class, and have the third finger of the Right hand upon B♭ or A♯, and the third finger of the Left hand upon G or F♯, or upon G♭ or F♯.

EXERCISE No. 30.

SCALE OF F MINOR.   Component Tones, F, G, A♭, B♭, C, D♭ or D♮, E♮.

SCALE OF B♭ OR A♯ MINOR.   Component Tones, { B♭, C, D♭, E♭, F, G♮ or G♭, A♮. / A♯, B♯, C♯, D♯, E♯, F♯ or F♯, G♯. }

SCALE OF D♯ OR E♭ MINOR.   Component Tones,   D♯, E♯, F♯, G♯, A♯, B♯ or B, C♯.
   E♭, F, G♭, A♭, B♭, C♮ or C♭, D♮.

SCALE OF G♯ OR A♭ MINOR.   Component Tones,   G♯, A♯, B, C♯, D♯, E♮ or E♭, F♯.
   A♭, B♭, C♭, D♭, E♭, F♮ or F♭, G♮.

THIRTY-SECOND RECREATION.

Directions.—This Recreation is played in two ways, as shown in full at (A), and as commenced at (B). In both, the chords are the same throughout, and are struck from the wrist in a flexible manner. At (A) all the tones are sustained by the fingers, which hold the keys the exact length of time indicated by the notes. The pedal is not used. At (B) the tones are sustained by the pedal, which is pressed simultaneously with the striking of each chord, and held down until the time for the next chord. It then rises to allow the dampers to act fully upon the wires. The hand uses the *staccato* touch, being drawn off and shut, as shown in Figure 21. The effect so produced is very different from that indicated at (A), or from any mode of playing by the fingers alone.

Figure 20.

The Hands prepared for a Staccato Chord.

Figure 21.

The Hands after striking a Staccato Chord.

THE STACCATO TOUCH.

§ 55. *Use of the Hand in Arpeggios.*— (§ 191, 4, p. 235.) The hand takes one position only in each octave, and is spread over the keys of each position as in the broken-chord exercises. Its movement from one position to another, as the Right ascends and Left descends, is two-fold. First: while the second or third finger is held upon its key, the thumb is bent under the hand, to reach the first key of the next position; and, as it is too short to accomplish this while the hand is unmoved, the wrist and knuckles are turned around in arcs of circles, whose center is the point of the finger that is held. Second: while the thumb is held, the hand is thrown over to its next position. The elbow is turned slightly outward, and the hand inward; but the arm is not rolled, nor the wrist elevated above its usual height. When the Right descends and the Left ascends, the change is reversed. Only by such a management of the hand, among all the tones of an

Arpeggio, can the legato be secured, perfect equality of power be attained, and great beauty and rapidity in such passages be acquired. Perfection requires that no *ear* shall be able to detect the place or mode of changing the hand, so that the following passage, for example, though fingered differently, shall sound precisely the same at (*a*) or (*b*) as at (*c*).

Figure 20.

EXERCISE No. 31.

Directions.—Place the Right hand in the first position indicated in Figure 21, and then, while holding the second finger upon the G-key, turn the hand around until the thumb can reach the C-key; thus make a perfect connection between the tones G and C. Bend all the joints of the thumb as it turns under. While the thumb is upon C, bring the hand to the second position. In descending, hold the C-key with the thumb, and turn the hand until the second finger can reach the G-key; thus make C perfectly *legato*. Train each hand separately, and persevere in this preliminary practice until all the changes can be made easily, while a perfect connection is maintained between the tones.

Figure 21.

The practice of the ACCENT EXERCISES UPON ARPEGGIOS should now commence with No. 173, p. 194.

THIRTY-THIRD RECREATION.

CZERNY.

MOLTO ALLEGRO. (1)

§ 56. Octaves.—Octaves must be played with a perfectly free wrist and flexible hand. When played with a stiff wrist and the use of the fore-arm, they are both disagreeable to the ear and fatiguing to the hands. Beginners are very liable to stiffen the wrists, especially if they attempt to play powerfully or rapidly before the hands are fairly accustomed to the extension required by octaves. In striking the black keys, large hands generally use the third finger.

No. 32. OCTAVE STUDY.

Directions.—Play slowly and softly at first, and be sure to have the curve of the fingers and the general position of the hand correct. Practice octaves only a few minutes at any one time, but recur to them very frequently.

(1) See Dictionary of Musical Terms, page 296.

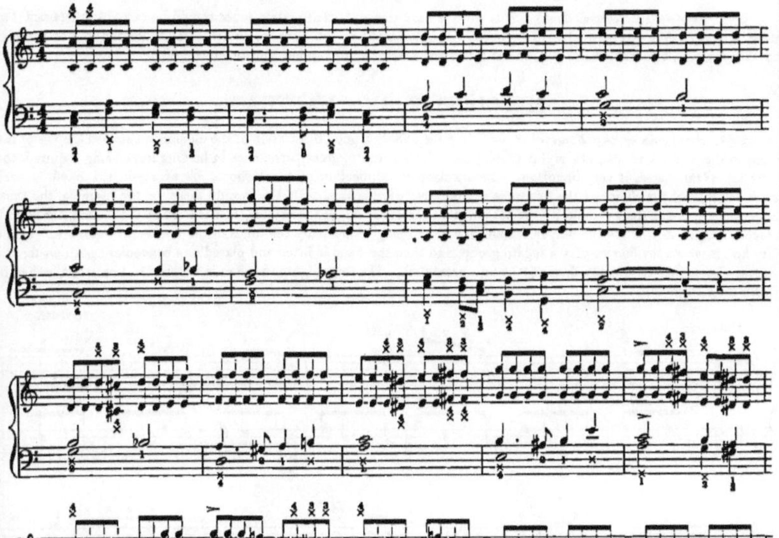
ritard.
dim.

§ 57. *Tenuto.* (*abbreviated* Ten.)—This word is used to signify that certain tones should be carefully sustained the exact length of time represented by their notes. It is indicated by the signs (∧) and (☐), and sometimes, inaccurately, by the *sforzando*, or accent-mark (➤), and still less accurately, by the accent sign reversed (◄).

MELODIES FROM "MARTHA."

§ 58. *Analysis of the Fingering.*—This piece affords a good illustration of the difference between the use of the hand in the legato and staccato styles of playing. In the legato, great persistence in holding keys being required, the selection of the fingers is very important. In the staccato, connection of tones should be avoided; the hand is used more freely, and the choice of the fingers is comparatively immaterial. In the twelfth measure, for example, the third finger silently takes the key held by the second, that the latter may be ready for the next tone; that taken, the thumb reaches a black key, while the fingers remain in place to play connectedly the tones of the fourteenth measure. In the fifty-first measure the fingers play a legato group, and then the hand is lifted and placed in a convenient position for the staccato tones that follow, the fingering being unessential. The forty-eighth measure is fingered in two ways, either of which may be chosen.

(1) This ♮, though unnecessary, is inserted, in accordance with the custom of composers, lest some should fail to notice the change of key.

§ 59. *The Damper Pedal,*—called by some the "Open Pedal," and by others, less properly, the "Loud Pedal,"—lifts all the dampers of the Piano Forte, and allows the wires to vibrate freely. It must, therefore, be used with great discrimination, to avoid a confused, discordant intermingling of sounds. The dampers must always be allowed to act fully upon the wires, at every change of chord. In modern music, PED. indicates the use of this Pedal, and ✳ its discontinuance. Some composers, even when the pedal is needed to produce the effects they intend, leave it wholly to the judgment of the performer.

§ 60. *The Action Pedal.*—The full tones of the Grand Piano Forte are nearly all of them produced by three strings in unison. A pedal is provided, which moves the key-board, or action, so that each hammer strikes only one string, or, in some instruments, two strings, and thus soft tones, of the same character as the loud, are produced. The soft pedal of the Square Piano produces a muffled tone, which is seldom agreeable. The use of the action pedal is indicated by *Una Corda,* abbreviated u. c.—one string; or by *Due Corde*—two strings. *Tre Corde*—three strings, shows that the action should be allowed to spring back to its usual place. That clear, sweet tone, with which some very skillful pianists occasionally delight their hearers, resembling the sound of a glass bell, is made by a very delicate use of the key and of both action and damper pedals.

LE ROSSIGNOL.

§ 61. *Analysis of the Fingering.*—The first eight measures of the Right hand part form a five-key passage, Ă to B̆. The next four measures form a six-key passage, Ă or B̆, B or C♯, D̆, Ĕ, F♯. After a few measures, which are fingered, a five-key passage, slightly varied, closes the strain. The Minor passage that follows can be analyzed by the learner. Upon the seventeenth page, a Broken-chord passage occurs, composed entirely of the Triad of E (Fig. 22). The hand takes three positions: the first, Ĕ, G♯, B̆, Ĕ, provides for seven tones; the second, B̆, Ĕ, G♯, B̆, for six, and the third, Ĕ, G♯, B̆, Ĕ, an octave above the first, for fifteen.

Figure 22.

In the next passage the slurs indicate accents upon the second and fifth parts of each measure, while the first and fourth parts are light and staccato; thus the regular grouping is broken up. (See § 26.) The hand rises after every staccato tone, and jumps to the next position. The fingering is as follows:

All the groups of sixteenths that follow, except the first, are commenced with the second finger.

The closing strain twice requires a silent change from the third finger to the first, and that the hand should be lifted after each staccato tone, thus:

Directions.—For preliminary practice, strike the chords as at B, Figure 22; then, in breaking them as at A, retain each position until the last tone is struck, and, while it is sounding, prepare by contraction for the next position. (See § 40, p. 45.)

LE ROSSIGNOL.

Allegretto.

F. HUNTEN. Op. 71. [1]

(1) Composers designate their works by numbers, in connection with the Latin word *Opus*, abbreviated *Op.* Some use the French word *Œuvre.* In purchasing music, the best way to describe the compositions of well-known authors is to give names and numbers simply. For example, "*Beethoven, Op. 26.*" When several pieces are included in an *Opus*, the number of the one desired should also be given. The Rondo, above, is "*F. Hunten, Opus 71, No. 3.*"

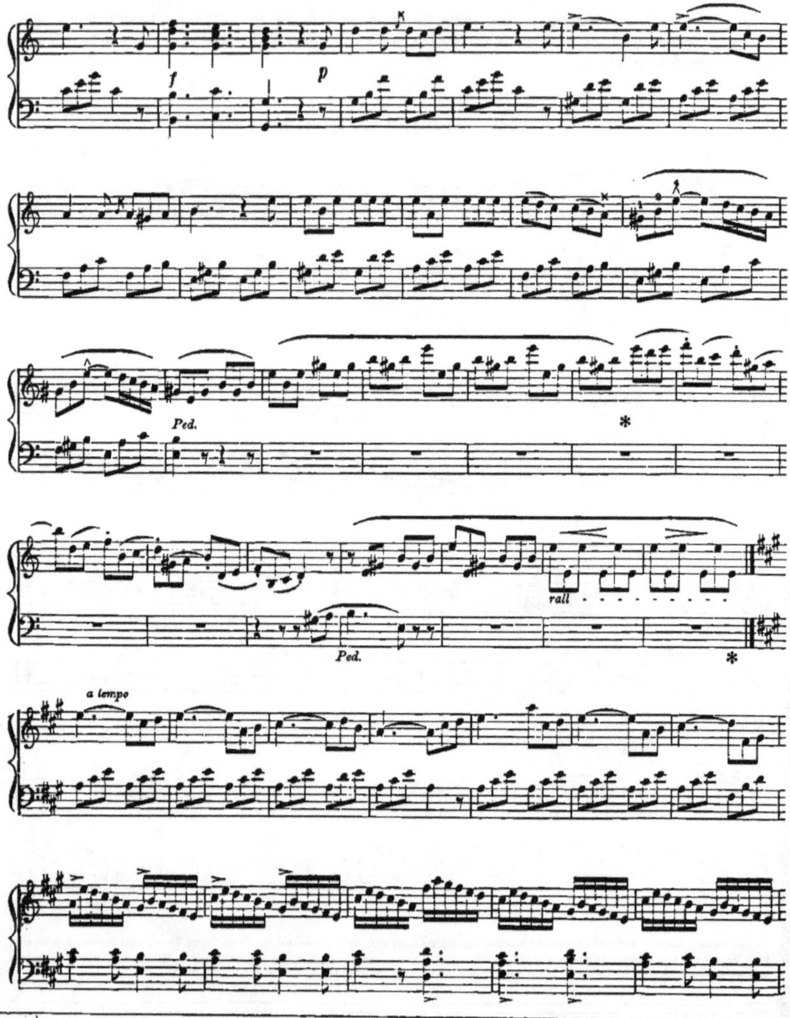
f
p
Ped.
*
Ped.
rall
*
a tempo

GENERAL PRACTICE.

§ 62. *Celerity.*—The pupil should now spend some time daily in practicing with the utmost celerity, remembering that slow playing, though indispensable for ensuring accuracy, even to the most accomplished pianists, will never give the power of executing rapidly. As one who would be expert in catching a ball, must learn to note its course, and shut his hand upon it vigorously at the right moment, so any one who would acquire skill in Piano-forte playing, must learn to decide instantly on the necessary positions of the hand and selection of the fingers, and must train the muscles to respond in like manner to the mental command. In acquiring celerity, the pupil must rush on through difficult passages, even at the risk of omitting some tones and mistaking some—at all events must play with speed. It *should be understood*, however, that this style of practicing, *if employed exclusively*—as indeed it is by many—will in a short time ruin any one's playing ; but taken in connection with constant practice of the most careful kind, it will produce gratifying and satisfactory results. Let the Five-finger exercises, then, and all forms of Scales, both Major and Minor, and the Broken-chords and Arpeggios, in all keys, receive in turn this kind of practice. To avoid neglecting any of them, a record should be kept of the various exercises of each day.

§ 63. *Dynamic Force.*—Regular and systematic practice of scales, and other exercises, is also now important for dynamic training. Each hand should play separately, and both together, in all the gradations of power, from *pianissimo*, which it is very difficult to acquire in perfection, to *fortissimo*, which, at times, should be produced by the boldest and firmest strokes, and at other times, by pressure, without lifting the fingers higher than is necessary to allow the keys to act. Also, one hand should play loud, and the other soft ; one *legato*, and the other *staccato*, with *crescendo* ascending, and *diminuendo* descending, and *vice versa*.

§ 64. *How to Learn a Difficult Piece of Music.*—Presupposing that the principles of notation and fingering are understood, the best mode of overcoming the difficulties of a Piano-forte composition is, substantially, as follows : The learner should at first try, four or five times, to play the whole piece slowly from beginning to end, to discover the more difficult passages ; he should then practice these *very slowly indeed*, counting aloud decidedly, and accenting the music very forcibly. When a passage has been so repeated, fifteen or twenty times, if it can be played alone, it should be tried in its connection. If still troublesome, it should not be practiced again immediately, but the hands should rest, or play some other part, and then recur to it again. Such management, which avoids impairing the tone and ,vigor of the muscles by too long practice in the same way, and is not insupportably wearisome, eventually overcomes all difficulties, and, after days, weeks, or months of practice, as the case may be, prepares the learner to play a long composition accurately throughout, and in its appropriate time. Proper practice of short passages has a far-reaching influence, rendering the whole habit of playing more accurate, and imparting certainty and well-founded confidence to the player. HASTE in attempting to conquer difficulties is fatal to success. When the mechanical difficulties connected with a mere production of the tones are so far overcome that due attention can be given to light and shade, all that pertains to the proper expression of the music should receive minute, thorough attention, and persevering practice.

§ 65. *Playing for Listeners.*—Learners should improve every opportunity to be heard by others, especially by such as are competent to judge of their performances. Though it is more difficult to play accurately in such presence, the concentration of mind required, the stimulus afforded, and the consciousness of intelligent approval, all tend to discipline and develop the pupil ; to impart freedom, ease, and grace. For this purpose it is well to commit entire pieces to memory.

ANDANTE FROM "WILLIAM TELL."

Directions.—In ¾ measure, when Triplets are frequent, the effect is that of ⁶⁄₈ measure ; but it is proper to trill in either way as the player chooses. This is illustrated by the two Trills that are written in full. All the Trills will require minute counting, one for each group of thirty-second notes, and much more practice than the other portions of the piece. The last group in the first Trill consists of a QUINTLET, called a TURN. (§ 77, p. 131, § 165, p. 231.) Several other similar Trills are indicated by *tr*, and small notes showing the termination of the Turn. The last two Trills have no Turn. They are accompanied by a melody, played by the Left hand, which should be very distinct, as indicated by the word *marcato*.

ROSSINI.

cres - cen - do.
sfz
pp staccato.
Ped.
crescendo.
sfz
p
marcato.
tr
ritard. e dim.
pp

§ 66. *Regular and Irregular Passages Combined.* —In many compositions for the Piano-forte, passages occur which require one hand to play regular groups of tones, while the other plays irregularly. Thus, for example, the Right hand may be called upon for two tones, while the Left plays three ; for four or eight tones, while the Left plays six; for seven, ten, thirteen, seventeen or twenty tones, while the left plays six, eight or nine, &c., &c. Such combinations are extremely difficult for those who have not acquired a certain independence in the use of the hands. They can be conquered by persevering endeavors, in the following manner :—1st. The hands should be practiced separately, until each can play its own part without difficulty. 2d. After one of the parts has been repeated several times, in immediate succession, while the mind is strongly impressed with it, and gives almost exclusive attention to it, the attempt should be made to play both parts simultaneously. 3d. The attention should be strongly fixed upon the other part, and the effort to combine the two repeated. 4th. Finally, both parts should receive equal attention.

WALTZ.

Directions.—The slurs, over many of the measures, require that the first, third, and fifth tones should be accented; and the second, fourth, and sixth unaccented and staccato. In playing the tenth measure, the Left hand is placed over the Right. (Fig. 35, p. 133.) The tones of the quintlet, in the nineteenth measure, should be equal in length. (See § 66.)

Attributed to WEBER, *but composed by* REISSIGER.

Da Capo al Fine.

Ped.   * Ped.   *   Ped.   *   Ped.   *   Ped.   *   Ped.   *

No. 33.   WRIST STUDY.

Directions.—All the tones of this study are to be played from the wrist, except five, which, being legato, require finger-touch. The staccato touch, described in § 36, p. 40, is to be employed only upon the eighth-notes, and the sixteenths that are followed by rests. The accented tones require a more forcible stroke than the others; and, in order that they may contrast strongly, all the unaccented tones should be soft. When the thumb is placed upon a black key, the hand must be further upon the key-board than at other times. In learning this study, the first thing is to practice adjusting the fingers quickly to the different positions required. When all these are familiar the training of the wrist may begin. The arm should be quiet throughout, the muscles all supple, and the motion perfectly easy. After the whole study can be played without error, it should be repeated several times daily until a high degree of speed is attained.

NIGHT'S SHADE NO LONGER.

Directions.— A clear understanding of the fingering will facilitate learning this piece. It should therefore be analyzed by the pupil with great care. For example: the third measure requires a five-key position, A̤—E̤, and the fourth, a six-key position, E̤—C. G♯, in the one, and D♯, in the other, are, of course, exceptional. In the first part of the twelfth measure an eight-key position, G—D, E, F, G, occurs, and in the fourteenth a seven-key position, G—C, D, E, F, &c., &c. In measures 19 to 32, inclusive, a melody and an accompaniment are played by the same hand. The melodic tones, marked *tenuto*, must be clearly struck and fully held. The hand must turn to enable the thumb to retain its key while the fourth finger passes over it. The thirds in the forty-first measure, and all the chords in the Left-hand part, are to be struck from the wrist in the most flexible manner. The thumb of the Left hand is placed upon both E and D, in the third chord of the forty-second measure. The embellishments may be omitted at first. (See § 77.) Practice slowly.

ROSSINI. *"Moses in Egypt."*

ALLEGRO.

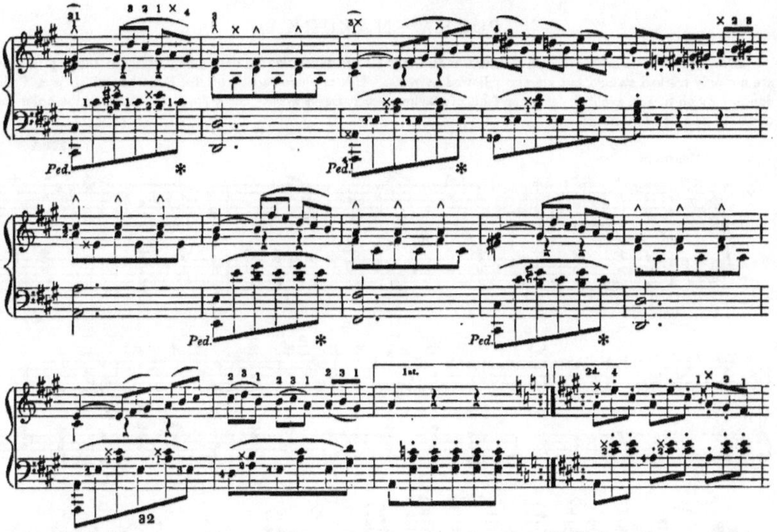
Ped.
Ped.
Ped.
Ped.
1st.
2d.
32
41
Ped.

POLKA—MAZURKA.

Directions.—Count six in each measure, until the rhythmic difficulties are overcome. Many of the eighth notes are not only marked *staccato*, but are also followed by rests. This is characteristic of the Mazurka, which is a Polish dance. By all means, avoid the common fault of playing such passages *legato*. See § 26, p. 23, and obey the order contained in every slur in this piece.

A. LEDUC.

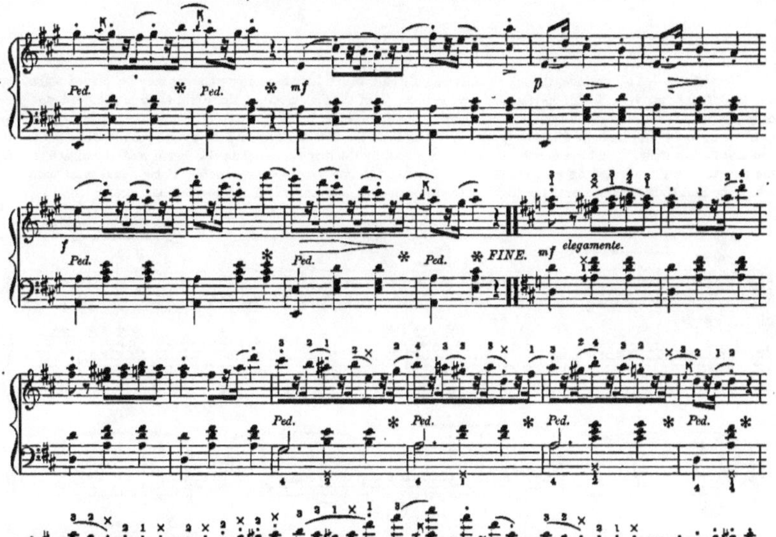
Ped.
mf
p
f
FINE.
elegamente.
delicato.
rf
D. C.

PRELUDE.

Directions.—This prelude, though peculiar and difficult, shows how harmonic passages may be played smoothly, and is quite instructive. While the fourth finger is upon D, in the first measure, the Right hand is extended, and prepared to connect that tone with the following chord. The third finger holds E, in the third measure, while the first rises to allow C♯ to be repeated simultaneously with A. The D, in the fifth measure, is held by the thumb, while the fourth and first fingers strike their keys above ; then the F♯ is held by the first finger, while the fourth and thumb strike. In the twelfth measure, C♯ and A♯ are both struck by the Right thumb extended over them. Some hands must omit the A♯. The Left thumb crosses over the Right in the first measure, and under it in the seventh measure.

F. CHOPIN. *Op.* 28, *No.* 7.

ANDANTINO.

THE DESIRE.

Directions. —Practice the first part of this piece as an exercise in connecting well the tones of a melody, while an accompaniment is played by the same hand. To do this, it is necessary, in several instances, to change fingers quickly and silently, upon a key that is held. Some places can be made *legato* only by large hands. The *turn* in the eighteenth measure is made thus : The ♮ below the sign ∾ indicates that D should be natural. (See §§ 77, p. 131, and 165, p. 231.)

Attributed to BEETHOVEN, *but composed by* SCHUBERT.

ALLEGRETTO.

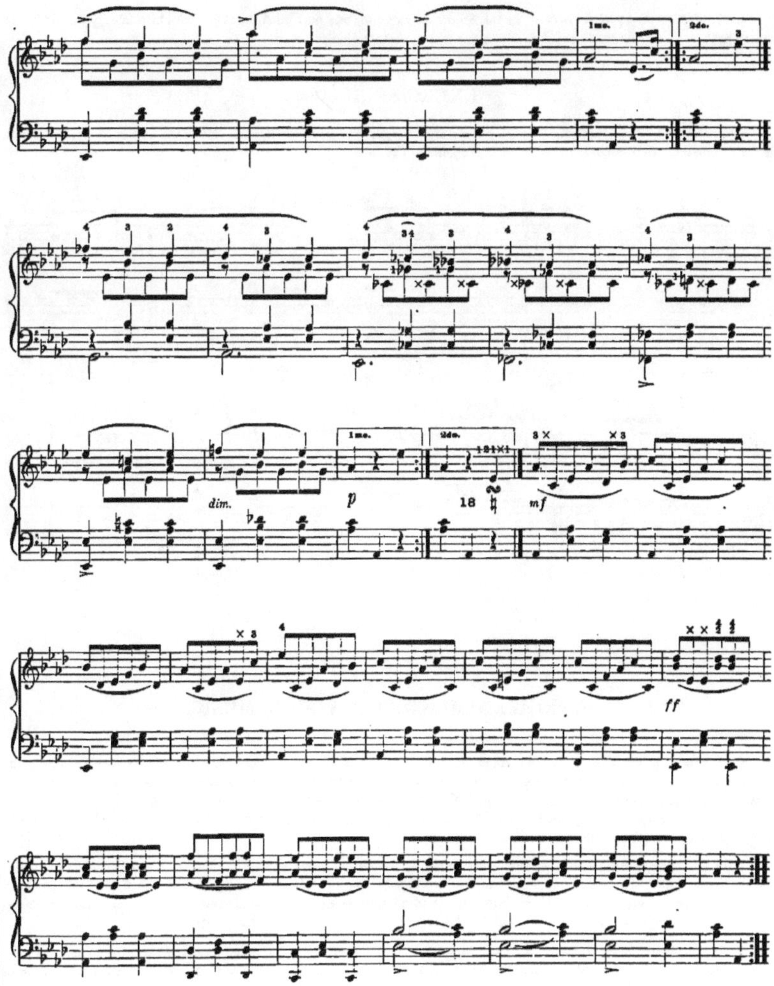
1mo.
2do.
dim.
p
18
mf
ff

§ 67. *Sixths Played Legato.*—In the following exercise, one part must, in every case, be made *legato.* In many places both parts can be made so; but in some it is quite impossible.

EXERCISE No. 34.

Directions.—Strike both keys exactly together. Begin with separate hands. Move the fingers freely, and avoid, as far as possible, all straining, twisting, or movement of the hand.

Play through two octaves.   *Play through two octaves.*

ACCOMPANIMENTS OF VOCAL MUSIC.

§ 68. Vocal music may be accompanied by the Piano-forte in either of two ways:—1st. By playing simply the tones that are sung. 2d. By playing other tones, in harmonious continuity, more or less elaborate. Compositions consisting of several successions of tones, performed simultaneously by different voices, and therefore called VOCAL PARTS, are generally, if simple, accompanied in the first manner. Songs, and the larger forms of all kinds of vocal music, usually 'have separate accompaniments.

§ 69. *In Accompaniments of the First kind,* the different parts should be played, as nearly as possible, as if each of them were a solo melody sung, rather than played, by the instrument. To produce the singing effect in perfection, all the tones must be *legato.* This, however, is often impossible, and in some cases, one part only can be played connectedly. Either part may answer; but the highest, on account of its prominence, should then be preferred.

§ 70. *In Four-part Music,* that part which has the highest pitch, is called the SOPRANO; the next lower, the CONTRALTO, or ALTO; the third in order, the TENOR; and the fourth the BASE. These parts are arranged in four different ways, in the Tune Books in common use.

Figure 23.

FIRST METHOD. SECOND METHOD. THIRD METHOD. FOURTH METHOD.

In all of these, the Right hand plays the Soprano and Alto parts, and the Left the Tenor and Base. When the Tenor is too high for the Left, it is taken by the Right, and when the Alto is too low for the Right, it is played by the Left. Occasionally a Tenor or Alto note is out of the reach of either hand : it is then taken by the Right, an octave above its proper pitch.

EXERCISE No. 35.

Directions. — Practice the following well-known Chant in the strictest *legato* style. It will be necessary, in several instances, to change fingers, quickly and silently, upon a key while it is held. Slurs over the figures indicate this. Where *three* figures are placed above the staff, the Right hand is to play the Tenor. When a key must rise, before the time of its tone expires, to prepare for repetition, (as the first in the Tenor,) the other part played by the same hand should, if possible, be *legato*. The fourth method of arranging the parts, being less difficult than the others, is taken first.

The ENGLISH NATIONAL HYMN may be less *legato*.

The First, Second and Third methods of arranging the parts are perplexing only at first. The *Tenor* is played an octave lower than it is written.

PORTUGUESE HYMN.

EXERCISE No. 36.

Directions.—This beautiful composition should be played very sweetly, and very *legato*. The duet between the Soprano and the Alto is repeated, note for note, by the Tenor and Base. Try to play as well with the Left hand as with the Right, and, while the Left has the melody, let the Right be so soft, that the Left may be distinctly heard. Some notes of the Tenor must be played by the Right hand; and there is one that cannot be played at all, except by large hands.

THE NIGHTINGALE.

FOUR-PART SONG.

MENDELSSOHN.

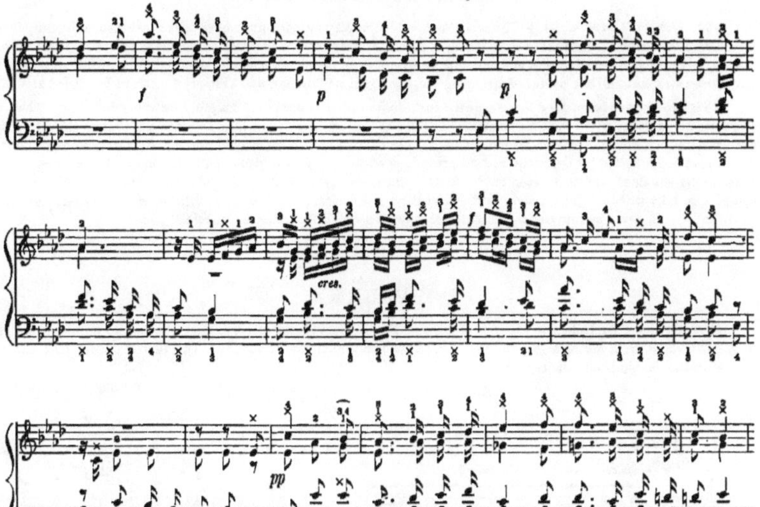

f
p
cres.
pp
R. H.

§ 71. *General Directions.*—The *principles* involved in playing part-music have been illustrated sufficiently by the foregoing compositions; but facility in this kind of accompaniment can be acquired only by long practice. The pupil who desires it, should play all the tunes and anthems in several of the books in common use, beginning with the less difficult, and persevering until all the modes of arranging the parts become familiar, and ordinary tunes can be played at sight.

§ 72. *Accompaniments of the Second kind,* do not differ materially from other instrumental compositions, and therefore no explanation of their mechanical difficulties is needed here. But they do especially require that the player should listen, not only to the accompaniment itself, but also to the singing; should notice and follow all deviations from the exact time indicated by the notes, and all gradations of power; should pause patiently upon note or rest while a tone is long sustained, and then recommence at the proper moment in the most effective manner; should, in short, sympathize fully with, and be led and governed by the vocal performance. Above all, when a solo is sung, the accompaniment should never be noisy or indifferent, either overpowering the voice, or inaudible.

MAZURKA.

Directions.—The Italian words, *Dal Segno senza Fine,* show that this peculiar Mazurka has no necessary end, but is to be repeated, from one sign (𝄋) to the other, at the pleasure of the performer. The thumb should take the first note after the double bar in the repetition.

F. CHOPIN. *Op. 7, No. 5.*

§ 73. *Notation of Complicated Passages.*—Much improvement has lately been made by LISZT, RAFF, and others, in the mode of writing complicated passages for both hands. The practice now is, to write all the notes to be played by the Right hand upon the upper staff, and all to be played by the Left upon the lower staff, with such changes of clefs as may be required. It is, however, to be regretted, that many composers are careless in this regard, and still write in a mixed, and more or less confused manner.

EXERCISE No. 37.

CHROMATIC SCALE IN OCTAVES.   THE RIGHT HAND ALTERNATING WITH THE LEFT.

Directions.—This mode of playing is governed by the eye, with no other thought than, simply, that the Left hand strikes three white keys, C, D, E, and three black ones, F♯, G♯, A♯, while the Right strikes two black keys, C♯, D♯, and four white ones, F, G, A, B, in each octave. For preliminary practice, it is well to try each hand separately, thus:

Then one hand may strike single tones, with either first or second finger, while the other hand plays octaves, as follows:

The Accent Exercises, Nos. 213 (p. 212) to 222, inclusive, should now be practiced.

§ 74. *The Tremolo.*—A trembling effect, produced in Piano-forte music by rapid reiteration or alternation of tones, is designated by the term TREMOLO. Many play Tremolos irregularly, and exert themselves unnecessarily in so doing; they therefore soon become confused and wearied. If played in perfect time, and with a flexible hand. such passages are not difficult. Tremolos are generally abbreviated, and are written and played as follows:

EXAMPLES.
Figure 24.

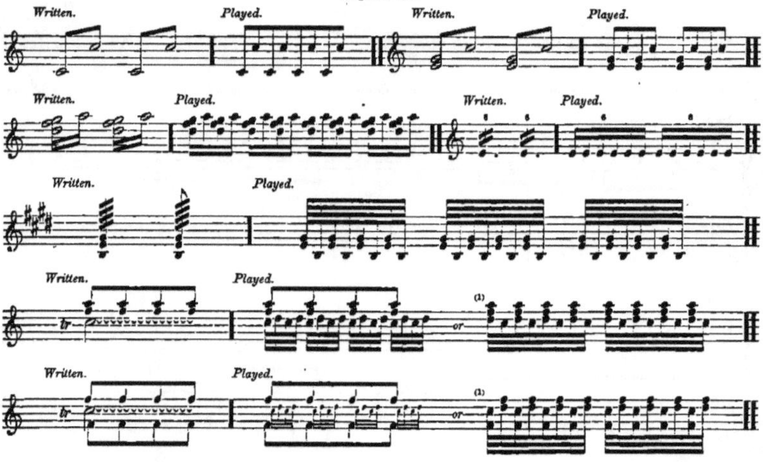

Written.   *Played.*   *Written.*   *Played.*

Written.   *Played.*   *Written.*   *Played.*

Written.   *Played.*

Written.   *Played.*   (1)

Written.   *Played.*   (1)

(1) This mode of playing is less in accordance with the idea of a Trill, as indicated by the abbreviated measure, than the first mode; but it produces a somewhat similar effect, and is not so difficult. Entire unanimity in regard to modes of writing and playing such passages does not exist among musicians.

FANTAISIE.

Directions.—The phrasing of the first four measures should be that indicated by the slurs. (See § 26, p. 23.) The accompanying chords in the next four measures should be struck lightly, with a supple hand and free wrist. The melody, beginning in the eleventh measure, should be clearly brought out by the Right hand, the long tones being well sustained. Draw off the hands from the keys in playing the *staccato* chords that form the accompaniment. In the twenty-sixth measure, the sixteenth notes, following the dotted eighths, are to be played in exact time, the triplets by the Left hand being quite independent. The *legato* sixths, in the thirty-sixth measure, should receive special attention. In the Cadenza following, the scales may be *ad libitum*. In the *allegretto* melody, each short note belongs to the following long one, and is to be closely connected with it. The melody commencing with the one hundred and sixteenth measure, requires great delicacy and finish to exhibit its beauties. The long tones should be fully sustained, and the pauses observed. The *tremolo* passage should be played by the fingers alone, the melody in the Base being distinctly brought out. All the characters indicating style, phrasing, or dynamic expression—in other words, all the *legato, staccato, tenuto,* and accent marks; the dots, ties, pauses, &c., must receive careful attention. Without a due observance of such characters, no well-written composition can be properly, or even respectably performed.

FANTAISIE.

"Don Pasquale." J. B. DUVERNOY. *Op.* 275.

con espress.
Ped.
marcatiss.
riten.
tempo 1mo.
accentato.
Ped.
8va
accentato.
espress.

rall.
piu f
piu f
dim.
a tempo.
ritard.
a tempo.
con espress.
36
8va
40
brillante leggero.
8va
piu f
cres.
ALLEGRETTO.

p
tempo riten.
tempo 1mo.
mf
dolce.
cresc.
dolce.
cresc.
cresc.
sf
sf
dolce con delicatezza.
8va

8va
piu f
dim.
cres.
8va
cres.
f
8va
sempre f
dim.
ritard.
MODERATO.
p
p
116

brillante.
piu f
leggiero.
piu f
leggiero.
piu f
f con fuoco.
marcato.
145
marcato.
cres. molto e animato.
f
f
f energico.
f
f
f
ff
ff

ANDANTE MOVEMENT.

Directions. — The accurate measurement of time in this piece is somewhat difficult. Count six, and carefully study every measure. As a general rule, all syncopated tones receive special stress. (§ 107, p. 226.) The accents, in this kind of measure, are placed thus :

| Countings, | 1, 2, 3, 4, 5, 6, | 1. |

Regular Accents,

Syncopation,

In the twenty-fifth measure, a passage commences in which the Left-hand part should be prominent. In some measures, each hand plays two parts, the long tones of one being sustained, while several short ones of the other are struck.

CZERNY. *Op.* 369, *No.* 25.

§ 75. *Doubly Marked Notes.*—When both *legato* and *staccato* marks are placed over a note, or group of notes, thus: each tone should be held nearly its full time, until the instant when the key must rise, in order to clearly disconnect it from the following tone. The tones of a group should be nearly equal in power.

MELODY AND SCALE.

Directions.—The following melody, with accompaniment in small notes, forms a pleasant and useful STUDY, not only in scale practice, but in transposition. It may be changed to the key of D, by supposing that the signature is two sharps, and playing accordingly. Each accidental natural will then be read as if it were a sharp. It may be changed to the key of C, mechanically, by taking, for every tone, the next key to the left of the one indicated by its note. After these two transpositions have been made, other keys may occasionally be tried, until, by perseverance, all the difficulties of transposition are overcome. Render the melody with perfect distinctness, and play the scale passages very lightly and evenly. In the second measure, the Right hand plays two tones of the scale, marked M. D., and is immediately followed by a chord, struck by the Left, marked M. G., the highest tone of which is melodic. These changes should not interrupt the continuity of the accompaniment. In the seventh measure, the Right hand should be passed under the Left.

FINE.

No. 38. STUDY.

Directions.—To play *legato* with one hand, and, at the same time, *staccato* with the other, is at first, difficult. It should be attempted very slowly, and with great care as to accuracy. When this study can be played well, as written, it will be very useful to practice it *staccato* throughout.

ALLEGRO ASSAI.

ST. HELLER, *Op. 46. No. 1. (Etudes progressives.)*

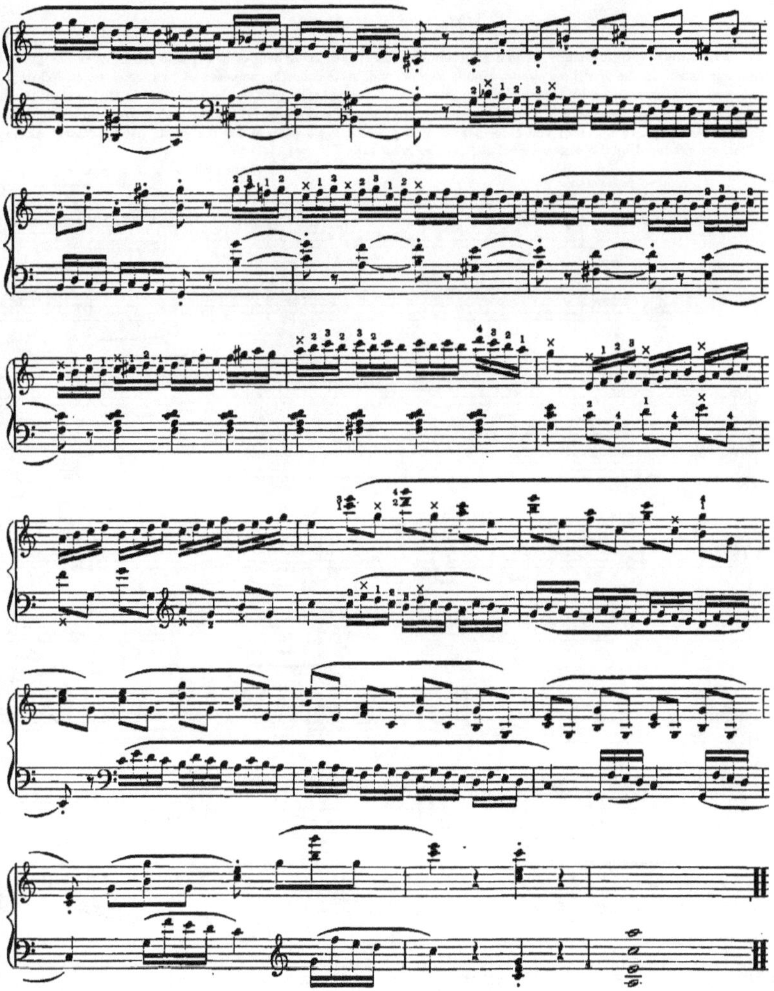

No. 39.   STUDY.

Directions. — In this study, certain tones are reiterated, each being held, as nearly as possible, its full length.   An accompaniment, in the first three strains, wholly *staccato*, and, in the fourth, composed of two *legato* tones, followed by one *staccato* in each measure, is played at the same time.   The chords struck by the Left hand in the seventh, twenty-third, thirty-first, and several other similar measures, are accented and *tenuto*, (§ 57, p. 66.) each being followed by *staccato* tones in resolution, (§ 183, p. 233,) and accompanied by a graceful *legato* passage for the Right hand.   Nearly all these effects are produced by the fingers alone, and require great care.

ST. HELLER.   *Op. 46, No. 3.* (*Etudes Progressives.*)

ALLEGRETTO SCHERZANDO.

HOME, SWEET HOME.

Directions.—This piece affords good practice, in so playing a melody, that it shall contrast strongly with its accompaniment. The melodic tones, written with large notes, are played *legato* and *tenuto*, in a clear, distinct, well shaded, fully sustained, and connected manner. The accompanying tones, written with small notes, are very light, and, nearly all of them, *staccato*. The effect produced is precisely that of two instruments, alike in quality of tone, one of which is prominently heard, while the other is but little more than audible. This two-fold effect can not be produced by a single player without long-continued, careful training, and repeated, persevering endeavors. Follow the fingering closely. In the seventeenth and eighteenth measures, play all the tones *as legato as possible*, and give special attention to the ties. When the Left hand is required to extend over more than one octave, as in the fifth measure, the lower tone is struck first. (See § 76, p. 110.) Count four.

SCALES IN DOUBLE THIRDS.

(See Theory of Fingering, § 189, 3, p. 234.)

EXERCISE No. 40.

Directions.—In playing the scales in double thirds, each hand can make one part only entirely *legato*. The other part must be more or less detached. Commence by descending with the Right hand. The lower part, then, may easily be made *legato*. Do not *break* the thirds in the least, in other words, strike them simultaneously.

Figure 25.

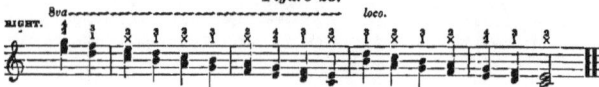

In *ascending*, the upper part is made *legato* by crossing the second finger over, while the fourth, or third, curls under to hold its key until the second strikes. In the key of C, G is held by the fourth finger; B, and afterwards D, by the third, and thus the upper part is played connectedly through the whole scale. In the lower part, E can not be *legato*, because the second finger must leave it to go over to A. All the other tones may be connected; for, while the first is upon G, the thumb can turn under to A; while the first is upon B, it can turn under to C. Be careful to strike the thumb exactly with the second finger.

Fig. 26.

When the third finger is upon a black key, and the second is to take a white, thus:

Fig. 27.

it is impossible, for some hands, to make the upper part *legato.* The first finger may then be held, while the thumb and second reach their keys, as follows:

Fig. 28.

The same principles apply to the Left hand. The *slurs*, in this exercise, show which notes are to be held to secure the *legato*, and the *dots* indicate which notes can not be held, but must be detached. It is unnecessary to learn all these scales at once. Two or three now—enough to accustom the hand to such use—will suffice. The others may be interspersed with the pieces that follow.

MAJOR SCALES IN DOUBLE THIRDS.

SCALE OF C.   *Fourth Finger of Right Hand on G. Fourth of Left on C.*

RIGHT, separately.

LEFT, separately.

SCALE OF G. *Fourth finger of Right hand on D. Fourth of Left on D.* (See § 87.)

SCALE OF D.   SCALE OF A.   SCALE OF E.

RIGHT HAND.

LEFT.

SCALE OF B.   SCALE OF F♯.   SCALE OF F.

SCALE OF B♭.   SCALE OF E♭.   SCALE OF A♭.   SCALE OF D♭.

MINOR SCALES IN DOUBLE THIRDS.

SCALE OF C.   SCALE OF G.   SCALE OF D.   SCALE OF A.

SCALE OF E.   SCALE OF B.   SCALE OF F♯.   SCALE OF C♯.

SCALE OF G♯.   SCALE OF D♯.   SCALE OF B♭.   SCALE OF F.

CHROMATIC SCALE IN DOUBLE THIRDS.

MISERERE FROM "TROVATORE."

Directions.—The chords in this piece require supple hands and free wrists. There should be a very marked difference between the melodic tones, and those of the accompaniment. The former should be clearly and distinctly brought out, well-sustained, and closely connected; the latter must uniformly be light and subordinate. The first melody commences in the ninth measure, the second in the eighteenth. All the notes indicating melodic tones are upon the upper staff, and have their stems turned upward. Count eight for each of the first sixteen measures, then, as triplets are frequent, and the effect is that of $\frac{12}{8}$ measure, count twelve, or six twice. After the difficulties arising from double dots, thirty-second notes, and triplets, have been overcome, count four for each measure, from beginning to end, to secure the same movement throughout.

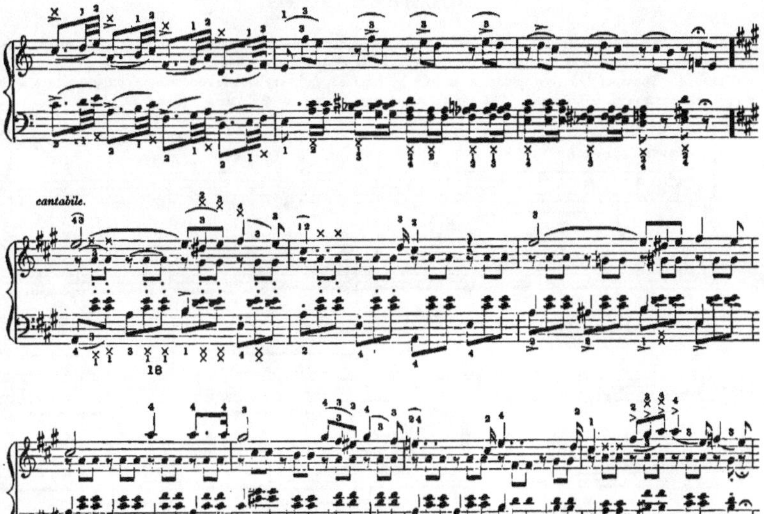
cantabile.
1mo.
2do.

SLUMBER SONG.

Directions. — The Left hand frequently strikes tones higher than those played by the Right. It is placed over the Right in all the measures except the last four. The tones of the melody should *sing*; should be distinct, clear, and well-shaded. Those of the accompaniment should be subdued, and very closely connected, flowing together, without accent, like the sounds of an organ. The damper pedal must be very carefully used. (See § 59, p. 68.)

ST. HELLER. *Op.* 81, *No.* 15. (*Preludes.*)

(1) These figures, in connection with the ♩, signify that this composition should be performed at the rate of 100 quarter notes in a minute of time. This rate may be obtained not only from the METRONOME, an instrument invented for the purpose of measuring time, but also from the simple swinging of a small weight, attached to a cord, held by the hand. If the length of the cord is two feet, the weight will vibrate at about the rate of 80 times per minute; if it is 17½ inches, 100 per minute; if 12 inches, 120, and if 9½ inches, 130.

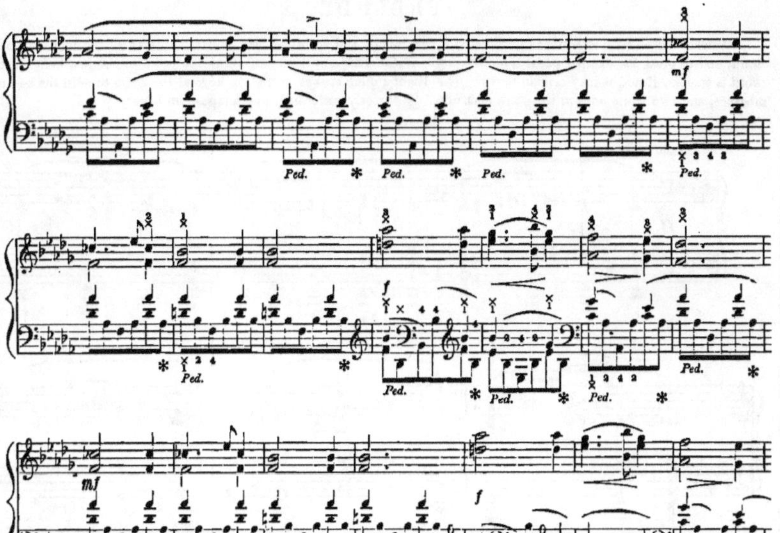
mf
Ped.
f
p
rall.
ritenuto.
pp

PRELUDE.

Directions. — Play as *legato* as possible with the fingers, and be particularly careful to strike all the tones of each chord, and to press the damper pedal *simultaneously.* If the harmony changes, allow the pedal to rise just before each chord is struck; if not, it may remain down.   The Right thumb strikes two black keys at the same time in the second measure, and two white ones in the sixth measure.   If properly performed, this composition is very grand.

F. CHOPIN. *Opus, 28, No. 20.*

LARGO.

HAUSMUSIK.

Directions.—The composer's direction, in regard to this beautiful little piece, is *einfach und innig ;* which may be translated,— *with simplicity and feeling.* The long tones should be fully sustained.

CARL REINECKE. *Op. 77, No. 1.*

§ 76. *Extended Chords* appear very formidable at first, but are really less difficult than they seem. Their component tones can not be struck quite simultaneously, but are rolled up from the lowest sound as rapidly as possible. This effect is indicated by a waved or curved line, thus :

Figure 29.

As written :

As played :

In playing them, the hand is first placed in a position to strike the lowest tones, and the fingers are extended as far towards the highest keys as ease, comfort, and flexibility permit. Then, as soon as the lowest tone is heard, the arm is suddenly moved to the right, the wrist is turned, and the fingers are brought to the upper keys. All chords that require only one extended position are thus easily struck. Others, like Figure 29 (*a*), demand the same use of the hand, with this addition, that, almost at the instant that the combined motion above described is made, the fingers are thrown over the thumb. The damper pedal is always used with such chords.

AMOROSA.

Directions.—In this piece the melody should be played very sweetly ; the *staccato* tones being clear and crisp, but not loud, and the *legato*, flowing, and delicately distinct. The chords played by the Left hand should be soft, as if accompanying a singer, yet they should be clearly heard, especially the sixteenths. The accompaniment written with small notes, and beginning with the thirty-third measure, should be limpid, light, and not sufficiently conspicuous at any time to draw attention from the melody, which is written with large notes. The fingering above the notes of the thirteenth measure is modern, (§ 82, p. 191) and is preferable to that below, which avoids the use of the thumb upon black keys. A passage commences with the forty-second measure in which the thumb has a succession of accents.

ANDANTINO.   JULES EGGHARD. *Op.* 157.

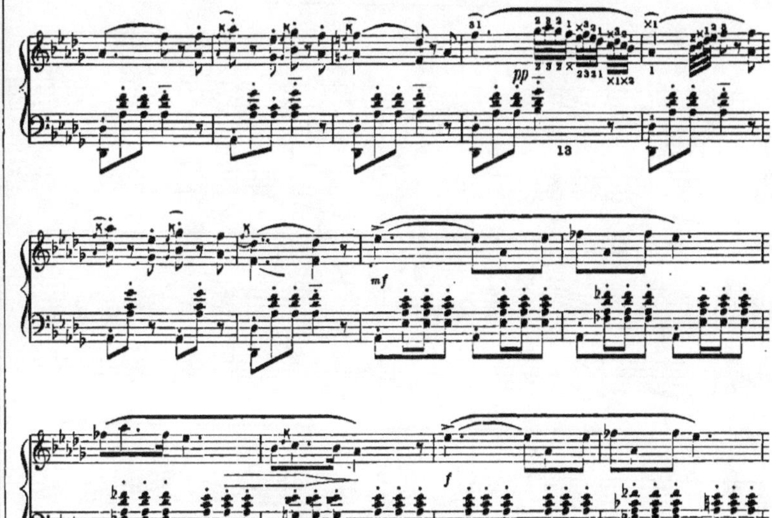
pp
13
mf
f
a tempo.
rall.
p
delicatamente.

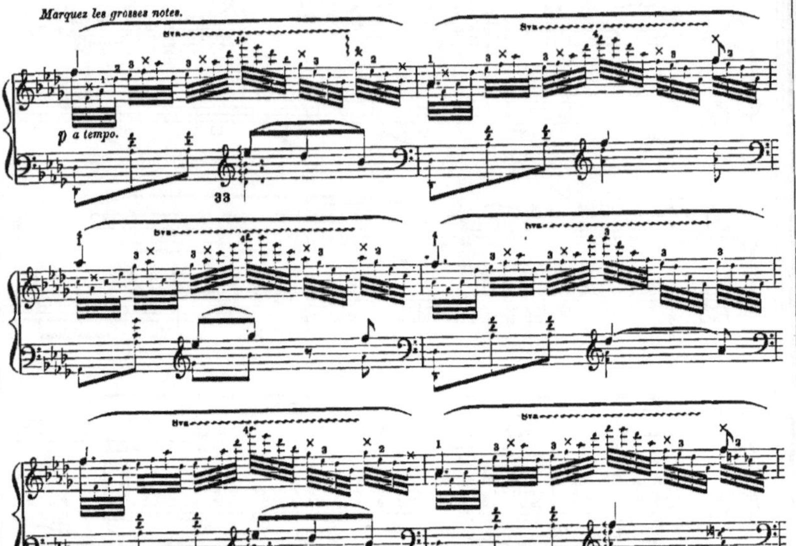
Marquez les grosses notes.
p a tempo.
33
dim. e rit.
a tempo.
p
42

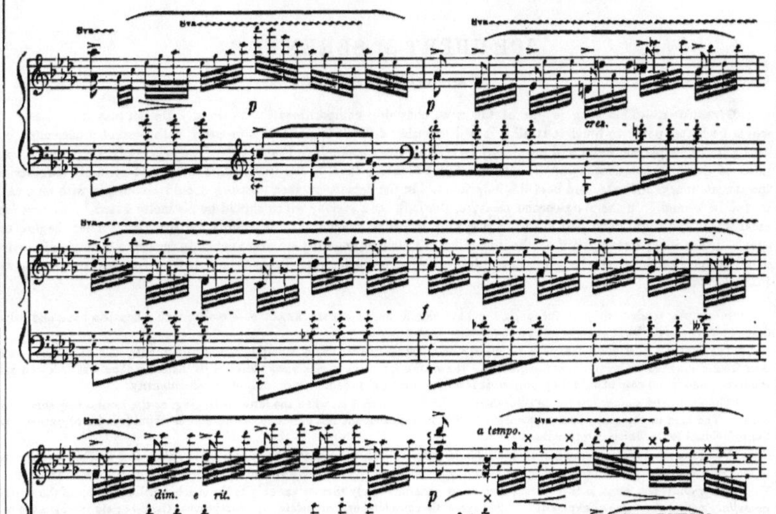
8va
p
cres.
f
dim. e rit.
a tempo.
M. D.
sempre
diminuendo.
pp

SCHUBERT'S SERENADE.

Arranged by S. HELLER.

Directions.—This song is one of the most charming compositions in the world.   Do not play it carelessly ; it would be better never to touch it at all.   It will be rather difficult to perform it properly, with present proficiency ; but finally it can be played well : and much may be learned from its study.   Practice the Base separately, until all the positions of the different chords can be struck without breaking them in the least.   Lift the fingers precisely together, as the *staccato* marks indicate, and hold the long tones.   In the repetition, each measure should commence with an octave by the Left hand.   In the sixty-second measure, the Left has a melody which should be distinctly heard.   The first four measures of the Right-hand part are to be played in the same manner as the chords for the Left.   Then begins the song.   Learn it separately, until all the difficulties of time and fingering are overcome.   In regard to the style of playing it, no better directions can be given than the following extracts from THALBERG'S "ART OF SINGING APPLIED TO THE PIANO-FORTE."

" In simple, tender and graceful songs, the keys should be, as it were, KNEADED, — moved with a boneless hand and velvet fingers ; they should be at such times rather CARESSED than STRUCK.

"The singing part should always be clearly and distinctly articulated, standing out as prominently as a fine human voice does from a subdued orchestral accompaniment.   The marks for *piano* or *pianissimo* placed with the song, should be followed only relatively, and in no case should they prevent it from maintaining its prominence, only with less intensity.

" The Left hand should always be *subordinate* to the Right — that is, when the latter is singing, as the reverse may sometimes occur.   The base or the accompaniment should be softened, so that the full harmony of the chords should be heard, rather than the individual tones which compose them.

" One important recommendation that we should not withhold, because it is one cause of the thin and ineffective character of melodies upon the piano, is to *hold* the notes and give to them (unless there are contrary directions) THEIR ABSOLUTE VALUE.

" We would also remark that young performers generally apply themselves only to the mechanical execution of the written notes, neglecting the signs of expression which serve to complete and translate the composer's thought ; signs which are to a musical composition what light and shade are to a picture.   In either case, if these indispensable accessories are omitted, there no longer exists either effect or contrast, and the eye, like the ear, is soon fatigued with the same coloring and the absence of variety."

" Those notes which are thus marked, ⊤ ⊤ ⊤, or ‿••••, are to be neither tied nor detached, but produced as they are by the human voice, the first ones a little more forcibly than the rest."

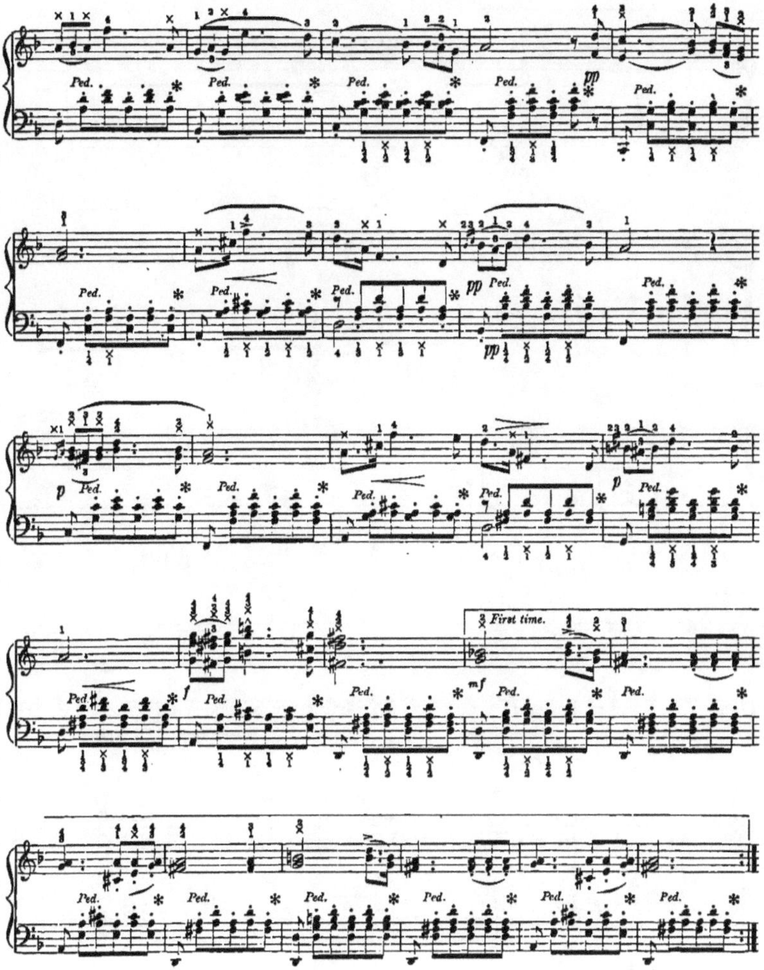
Ped.
pp
p
f
First time.
mf

Second Time.
Cres.
Ped.
62
fp
Ped.
p Doux.
p
Ped.
f
Decres.
Perdendosi.
pp
Les 2 Ped.
Dimin.

ALLEGRO MOVEMENT.

Directions.—This piece requires special care in phrasing. For example: the first phrase includes the first measure and one tone of the second. The upper part is all *legato*, except the last tone, and the lower has a *staccato* tone, rest, tied chord, and another *staccato* tone. After a rest, the second phrase begins with tied chords for both hands, the whole being included under a *legato* mark. There are numerous short phrases, commencing with accents, and included under *legato* marks. All the phrases should be made perceptible to the ear. The appoggiatura of three tones, in the twenty-sixth measure, should be closely connected with the following chord. (§77, p. 131.) The rests, *legato*, *staccato*, accent, and dynamic marks, and the fingering, require the closest attention.

Allegro con grazia.   WOLDEMAR BARGIEL. *Op.* 22. *No.* 1.

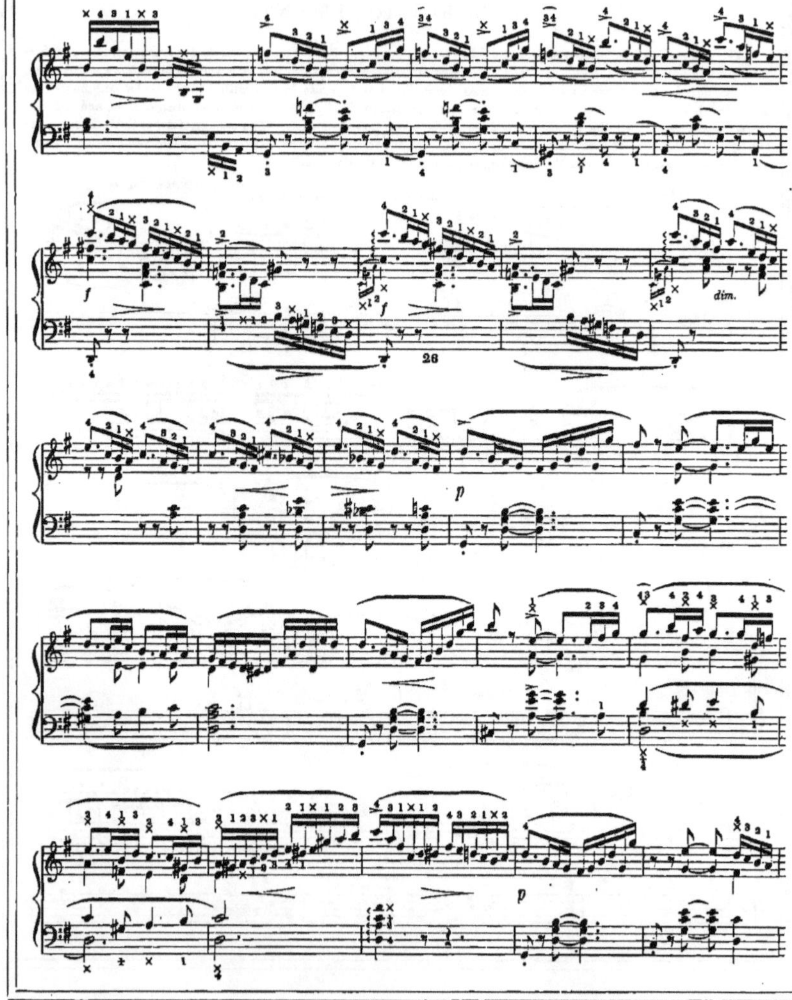
dim.

CRADLE SONG.

Directions. —The broken-chord accompaniment of this melody is played by the Left hand, excepting a few tones that are more conveniently taken by the Right, and are therefore written upon the upper staff. The first of these is f, in the fourth measure, and is struck by the thumb. In the eighth measure, while the fourth finger holds e♭, the thumb reaches f, and the first and second fingers play a♭ and b♭; then, while those tones are held, the fourth finger moves down to d. In the ninth measure, the first finger silently changes with the fourth upon b♭ to connect with g. In the eleventh measure, the third holds c, of the accompaniment, while the fourth slips down to d. Thus the tones are constantly connected. The upper part, in the nineteenth measure, is composed of groups of two tones, each three sixteenths in length, thus :

In the twentieth measure, the thumb of the Left hand passes under the Right. The twenty-third measure has three parts for each hand, which require great care in regard to the fingering. In the forty-second measure, the thumb of Left plays three keys in succession, the D, in the lowest part, being struck with the e♭ above. Constant attention will be required to the ties, *legato* and *staccato* marks, and to the strong contrast that must be maintained between the melody and the accompaniment. Repeat the first thirty-nine measures, and then, omitting thirteen, pass to the fifty-third, and close.

R. SCHUMANN. *Opus* 124, *No.* 16.

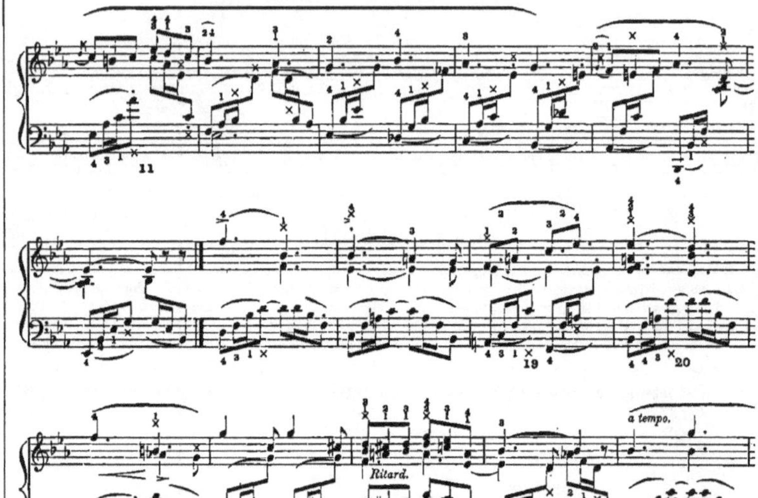
Ritard.
a tempo.
Ped.

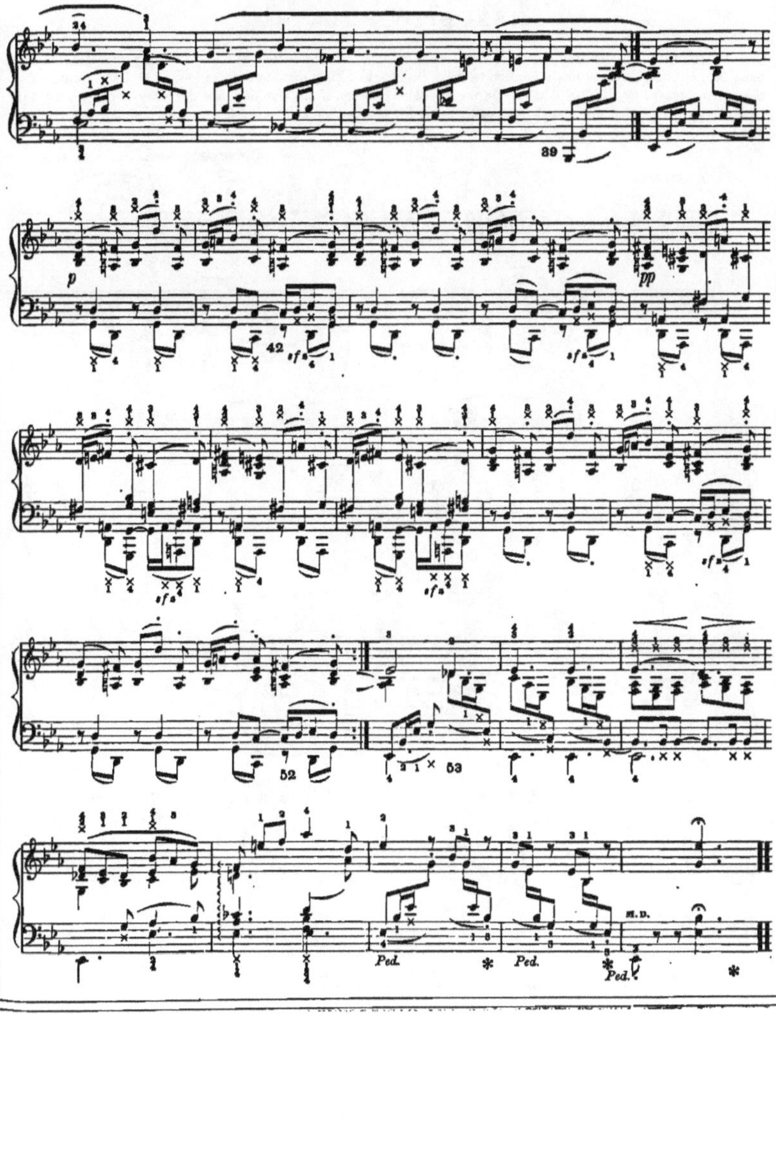
39
p
42
sfz
pp
52
53
Ped.
M. D.

MENUETTO AND TRIO.

Directions. — in crossing the Left hand over the Right, in the seventeenth and following measures, the wrist must turn to bring the hand into a position to strike the chords. They should not be so loud as to draw attention from the melody played by the Right hand. In the fifty-third measure, if the fingering over the notes be chosen, the hand must be so placed that the thumb may easily reach E♭, and the first and second fingers must play between the black keys. (See § 82, p. 191.)

F. SCHUBERT. *From Sonata in E flat, Op. 122.*

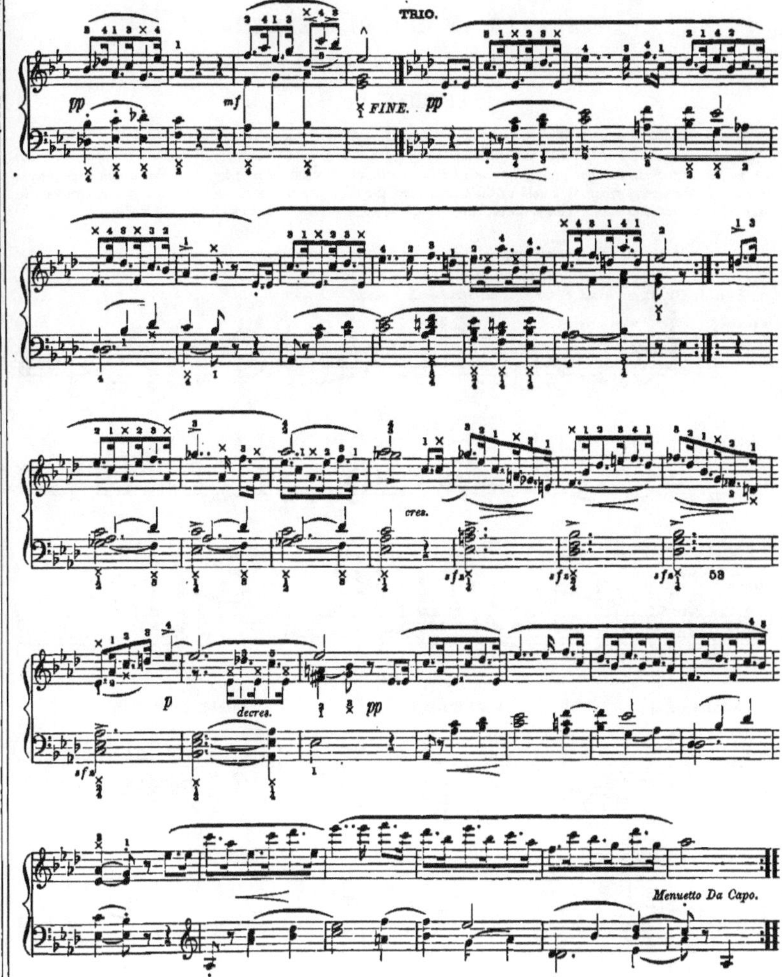
TRIO.
pp
mf
FINE.
pp
cres.
sfz
53
p
decres.
pp
Menuetto Da Capo.

SCALES IN DOUBLE SIXTHS.

(See Theory of Fingering, § 189, 5, p. 234.)

EXERCISE No. 41.

Directions.—In playing the scales in Double Sixths, each hand can make one part only entirely *legato.* The other part must be more or less detached. In this exercise, the slurs show which tones can, and the dots which can not, be connected. In the first group, D is held by the fourth finger, which curls under, while the second finger passes over it. In the second group, G is held by the fourth while the third passes over it. And so on. It is unnecessary to learn all these scales at once. Two or three, now, enough to accustom the hand to such use, will suffice.

MAJOR SCALES IN DOUBLE SIXTHS.

SCALE OF C.   *Second Finger of Right Hand on E.*   *Second of Left on G.*

SCALE OF G.   SCALE OF D.

SCALE OF A.   SCALE OF E.   SCALE OF B.

SCALE OF F♯.   SCALE OF F.   SCALE OF B♭.

SCALE OF E♭. SCALE OF A♭. SCALE OF D♭.

MINOR SCALES IN DOUBLE SIXTHS.

SCALE OF C. SCALE OF G. SCALE OF D.

SCALE OF A. SCALE OF E. SCALE OF B.

SCALE OF F♯. SCALE OF C♯. SCALE OF G♯.

SCALE OF E♭. SCALE OF B♭. SCALE OF F.

CHROMATIC SCALE IN DOUBLE SIXTHS.

"IF I WERE A BIRD."

The following well-known, and much admired composition, appears here with a new fingering, which materially lessens its difficulties. Nevertheless, it will require long-continued, patient and careful practice to master it. The learner will, however, gain largely in skill by it; and the beauties of the music will amply repay the effort. Instead of an alternation of four tones by the Right, and four by the Left, as in the original arrangement, the Right constantly assists the Left, and thus relieves it from many awkward positions. This use of the hand forcibly illustrates Rule I, § 188, p. 234. Compare Figure 30 with the new arrangement.

Figure 30.

ORIGINAL ARRANGEMENT.

First two measures.   M. G.   &c.

Seventeenth measure.   &c.

"Si oiseau j'étais,
A toi je volerais."

A. HENSELT. Op. 2, No. 6.

Con leggierezza quasi zeffiroso.

ALLEGRO.

pp

M. G.

legatissimo.

Ped. a chaque mésure.

FIRST TIME.
SECOND TIME.
M. D.
M. G.
17
pp
con espressione.
poco riten.

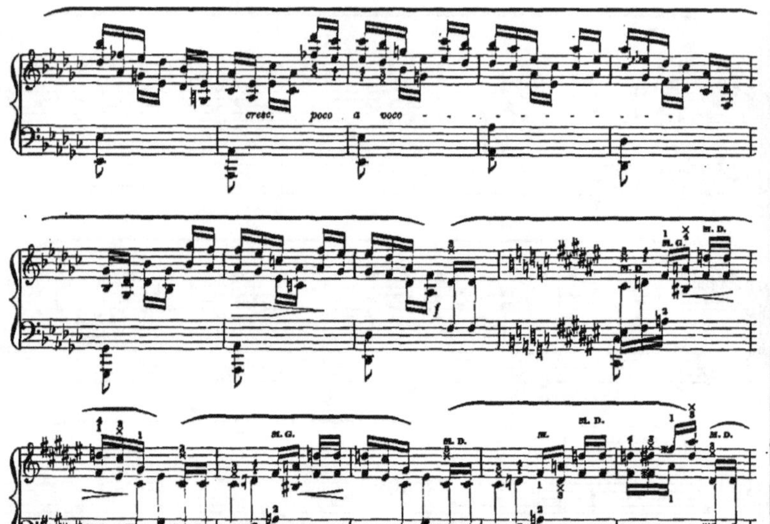
cresc. poco a poco
f
M. G.
M. D.
ff
con tutta la forza.
ff
Ped.
*

Tempo primo.
ff
ri- te- nu- to.
pp
p
f
dim. e rall.
a tempo.
poco riten.
a tempo.
pp
a due corde.

a tre corde.
poco riten.
pp
cres. con anima.
dim. e dolce.
cres.
con
calore.
cres.
f
dimin.
rall.
Lento.
Ped. * Ped. * Ped. * Ped. *

EMBELLISHMENTS.

§ 77.—1. An APPOGGIATURA of two or more tones (§ 162, p. 230,) is played, like a Single Appoggiatura, very lightly, quickly, and in close connection with the accented tone which follows it. In old music, many embellishments, having more or less the character of Appoggiaturas, were indicated by signs, and much diversity and confusion have arisen as to the true mode of interpreting them.[1] They are now generally written with small notes, which are easily understood. Figure 31, (a) exhibits the DOUBLE APPOGGIATURA. In many passages, marked *tr*, but too rapid to admit of a proper trill, the Double Appogiatura is employed, as at (b).

Figure 31.

(a)

Written.

Played.

(b) ALLEGRO.

Written.

Played.

In the following, and similar passages, the groups of small notes are analogous to Appoggiaturas.

Written.

Played.

(1) Although the doctrine of this book, in regard to APPOGGIATURAS, differs from that generally maintained, it is believed to be fully sustained by the playing of the best Pianists. The common statement, that Appoggiaturas, though unaccented, are yet played upon the accented parts of measures, and take their time from the essential tones following them, seems to have resulted from the fact that the small notes which indicate them are so written. Perhaps the so-called Long Appoggiatura, which was formerly written with a small note, but which in performance received an accent, and occupied half the time of the following large note, may also have occasioned some confusion. The Double Appoggiatura has certainly often been confounded with the Mordent.

2. The MORDENT is an embellishment which differs from the Double Appoggiatura in having the accent placed upon the first of the ornamental tones. It is always indicated by a sign, thus:

Figure 32.

THE DOUBLE APPOGGIATURA.   THE MORDENT.

It should not be played as a triplet, thus:

The Mordent derives its modern character largely from the works of CHOPIN; and the following extract from his well-known "*Impromptu*" is a good illustration of its use.

3. The TURN, as now indicated by the sign (∾), is, properly, an AFTER-TONE. (See §§ 163 and 165, p. 231.) It generally consists of four tones, which are played more or less rapidly, according to the movement of the composition in which it occurs. A sharp, flat, or natural, placed over the sign, effects the higher of the ornamental tones: placed below the sign, it effects the lower tone.

Figure 33.

When upon a dotted note, the principal tone is played after the Turn, in the time indicated by the dot, thus:

Turns are generally fingered with the second finger upon the essential or principal tone.

4. The TRILL, or SHAKE, has already been practically illustrated in connection with the *Andante from* "WILLIAM TELL." (Page 72. See also Fig. 24, p. 88.) When a Trill accompanies a melody, each melodic tone takes the place of one of the Trill tones, and thus is made perfectly distinct without interrupting the continuity of the Trill. Figure 34, an extract from THALBERG'S "HOME, SWEET HOME," exhibits this.

Figure 34.

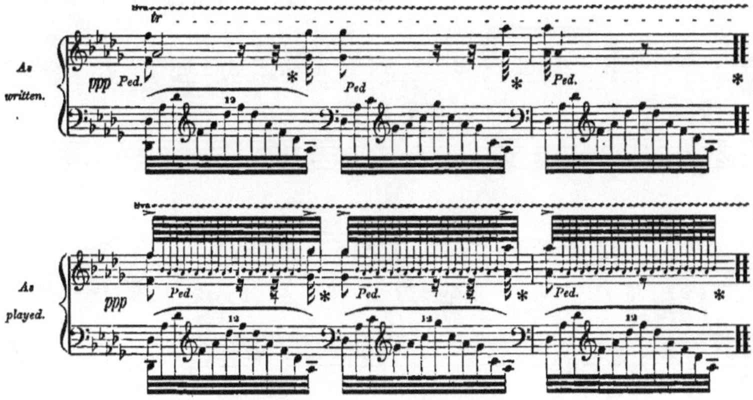

INTERLOCKING PASSAGES.

A few specimens of passages, in which continuity is maintained by one hand passing over and alternating with the other, are here presented. Although originality is not claimed for the principle involved, yet some of the following illustrations of it are new, and now for the first time published. BACH, and his cotemporaries, sometimes applied this principle to scales and simple arpeggios. In modern times, the application of it to more complicated harmonies has produced a variety of new and startling effects. E. HARBERBIEN was one of the first to elaborate such passages, showing great ingenuity and fertility of invention.

§ 78. *Analysis and Directions.*—In playing these passages, the hand which is required to strike more black keys than the other, should be placed above it.

Figure 35.

Great care is requisite that the changing of the hands may be imperceptible to the ear. Practice those tones that are within reach of the fingers, while the body of each hand remains unmoved, before passing from one octave to another. Interlocking passages may be greatly varied by changing the place of the accent.

Nos. 42, 43, and 44 are introduced to show the progress of art, and require no special explanation.

No. 42.

J. S. BACH. *From Concerto in D Minor, for three Pianos.*

No. 43.

J. S. BACH. *From the same Concerto.*

No. 44.

J. S. BACH. *From the same Concerto.*

In order to comprehend the modern interlocking passages, Nos. 45 to 55 inclusive, it is important to distinguish between the harmonic tones, that belong to the chords employed, and the accessory tones, which, though essential to the effect, do not form a part of the harmony. No. 45 is formed from the triad of F♯ Minor; the harmonic tones being F♯, A, C♯, and the accessory G♯, B♯, and E♯. The notation conforms to the principle explained in § 73, p. 86. Fig. 38 exhibits this passage divested of its accessory tones.

Figure 38.

No. 45

The Left hand over the Right. W. M.

No. 46 is composed of the triad of D♭ Major; the harmonic tones being D♭, F, A♭, and the accessory G♭ and B♭.

No. 46.

The Left hand over the Right. W. M.

No. 47 is composed of the dominant seventh chord, in the key of B♭; the harmonic tones being F, A, C, E♭, and the accessory G♭, A♭, and E♮.

No. 47.

The Left hand over the Right.

W. M.

No. 48 is formed from the dominant seventh chord in E♭; the harmonic tones being B♭, D, F, A♭, and the accessory A♮, C♭, C♮, C♯, D.

No. 48.

The Left hand over the Right in ascending, and under it in descending.

E. HABERBIER. *From Opus 1.*

CADENZA.

No. 49 is composed of the dominant seventh chord in F ; the harmonic tones being C, E, G, B♭, and the accessory B♮, D♭, E♭. The descending portion of this passage is slightly complicated by double tones, occasionally occurring, all of which are harmonic.

The Left hand over the Right. No. 49. W. M.

All the foregoing modern passages are modified arpeggios.

No. 50, after a trill upon I., proceeds with the scale of G Major. The arpeggio that follows is the triad of G Major, modified by the accessory tones, E, C♯, F♯, and A♯.

No. 50.

The Left hand over the Right in ascending, and under it in descending. E. HABERBIER. *From Opus 1.*

The next passage introduces the chromatic scale, and, after it, the triad of F♯ Minor, with D and B♯ as accessory tones.

The Left hand over the Right.

No. 51.

E. HABERBIER. *From Opus 5.*

The following example is formed from the diminished seventh chord, E♮, G, B♭, and D♭, with A♮, A♭, C, F, and F♯ as accessory tones.

No. 52.

The Left hand over the Right in ascending, and under it in descending.   E. HABERBIER. *From Opus 1.*

The first part of No. 53 is composed of two distinct harmonies; the triad of F Major being principal, and successive tones of that of G♭ Minor being accessory. The last part is the dominant seventh chord in B♭, with G and E♮ as accessory tones.

No. 53.

The Left hand over the Right in ascending, and under it in descending.   W. M. *From Opus 11.*

No. 54 also contains two distinct harmonies; the G Major triad being principal, and the F♯ Major triad, accessory. This is clearly exhibited in the closing measures, but is less perceptible in those composed of thirds.

The Left hand over the Right.

No. 54.

W. M.

molto cres - cen - do.

sempre ff e brillante.

Ped.

The following example is composed of the scale of C, in alternate thirds and sixths, and the scale of B, in thirds.

No. 55.

The Left Hand over the Right.

ANDANTE.

Directions.—There are several Turns and Trills in this piece, indicated simply by signs. Those that require explanation are written in full in Figure 39. The numbers under the staff correspond to those of the measures.

Figure 39.

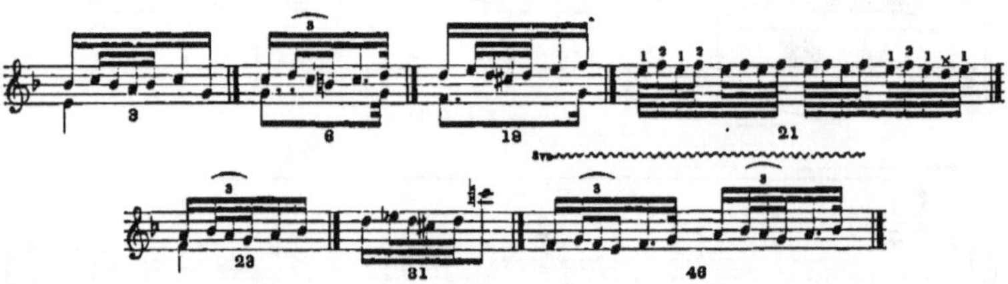

This whole piece demands the most patient and attentive study. It is a charming composition, and if played artistically, gives great delight to hearers who have sufficient culture to understand and appreciate its beauties. It would be better never to attempt its performance, than to neglect the *legato* and *staccato*, the long tones, or the delicate shadings of dynamic expression. Repeat the first twenty-two measures, and then, omitting thirty-two measures, pass to the fifty-fourth, and close.

ANDANTE.

MOZART. *Arranged by* F. BENDEL.

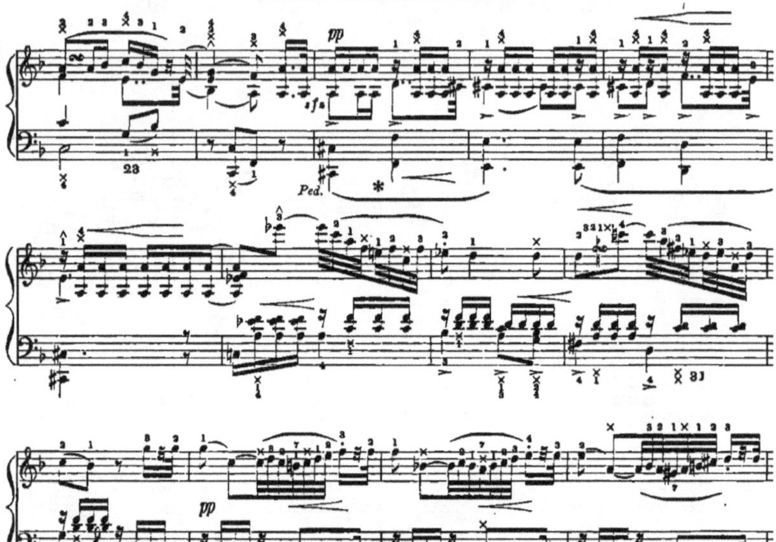
pp
sfz
Ped.
pp
p
tr
dim.

pp
staccato
p
46
51
54
ritard.
a tempo.
cres - cen - do
sfz
f
dim. molto
a tempo.
morendo

ACCENTUAL TREATMENT OF EXERCISES.

INTRODUCTION.

§ 79. *The Importance of Accentuation.* — Music consists, not alone in certain successions of tones, but in such a mode of producing them as is pleasing, interesting, and attractive. Audible reading, that lacks emphasis and pauses, is monotonous, unintelligible, and therefore tedious : so music that is destitute of accent, and of light and shade, attracts no attention, and produces no pleasing effect. There are persons who play the Piano-forte in a manner so enthusiastic, and so full of magnetism, that their music appeals directly and powerfully to those who hear it, creating intense delight. Others may play the same composition upon the same instrument, with as great, or even greater mechanical accuracy, and yet fail utterly to interest their hearers, or to awaken any emotion. Making all due allowance for individual peculiarities of touch, it is found that *those who accent well* are successful performers : they thus light up, and inspire their music ; while those who neglect accent are unsuccessful. It is, therefore, of the highest importance to acquire early the finger-power of accenting strongly those tones, which, for the sake of musical effect, should receive special stress. Another equally important reason for the practice of accentuation is, that by it, the strength of the fingers is most effectually equalized and increased. All the muscles and tendons of the hand and fingers need training and development ; and, in order to that, they must be used with frequency and vigor. THE MODE OF USING ACCENTS shown in this work, has never before been published ; but it has been thoroughly tested in private teaching, and has proved itself the most valuable training yet devised. By its aid, indispensable exercises are rendered less tedious ; pupils are able to play without depending upon written music — a great advantage in all finger-training — are beguiled into an amount of practice that ordinarily they will not bestow, and are able to compose new exercises, and thus add to practice some, at least, of the interest and pleasure of improvisation. Each finger is required to give sudden and strong accents, and every possible mode of succession is employed. These exercises have a most admirable disciplinary power, securing concentration of mind, and overcoming the tendency that many have, to stumble and fail after playing well for some time. They also aid greatly in acquiring celerity of execution. In addition to these great advantages, this use of accent furnishes most valuable assistance in overcoming all kinds of RHYTHMIC DIFFICULTIES, and gives learners practical training in KEEPING STRICT TIME, and in PHRASING. The benefit resulting from the practice of FIVE-FINGER EXERCISES — so universally and so wisely recommended by the old masters of Piano-forte playing, CLEMENTI, TOMASCHECK, HUMMEL, SCHMIDT, and many others, and by later writers, better known in this country, CZERNY, HERZ, BERTINI, and HUNTEN, — of SCALES, ARPEGGIOS, and, in fact, all passages of whatever sort, when considered as exercises, by this accentual treatment, is made complete. Accentuation exhausts the capabilities of exercises.

§ 80. *The Principles Involved are these:* — 1. That every succession of equal tones may be varied by introducing strongly marked accents with regular recurrence — one for every four tones, or some multiple of four, as eight, twelve, sixteen, &c., or one for every three tones, or some multiple of three, as six, nine, twelve, eighteen, &c. 2. That when a succession, so accented, is employed as an exercise, it may be varied still further by throwing the stress upon different tones — beginning to accent upon the second, third, fourth, or any other tone of the series, thus giving it a new interest, and increasing its value as an exercise. 3. That such successions, when continuously repeated within certain limits, until the accent recurs to the same tone and part of the measure with which it commenced, form, in some cases, very long exercises, which are interesting to the end, and are therefore of priceless value in training the hands. Exercises, applying these principles to each of the three great classes of passages described in §186, p. 234, have been composed for this work. The accented tones are indicated by large notes marked with double *sforzando*, thus : (♯) that they may readily be seen.

§ 81. *Suggestions to Teachers.* —Teachers are urged to give the subject of accentuation close and thorough attention, and to test the exercises in precise accordance with the directions given. The result will fully justify all that has been said in their favor. As far as possible, they should be described orally to the pupil, so much information only being given at each lesson, and such exercises, or parts of exercises, as may be needed at the time. The easier ones of each class should be first selected, and the difficulties gradually increased as the pupil acquires skill and can overcome them. The less frequent accents,—more perplexing and difficult than the more frequent,—should be reserved until command has been acquired over the latter. They are introduced together to show the development which characterizes these exercises. The diversity among learners is so great, that no definite rules for selection can be given; yet it may be said, in general, that the easier exercises of the first class should be used, while that portion of the book which precedes § 36 is being learned; then the easier exercises upon the chromatic and diatonic scales and broken chords should follow; later, the arpeggios should receive attention, and finally, in connection with the more difficult pieces, all the exercises having occasional accents should be thoroughly practiced *at the highest speed.* The accented tones should be struck with all the force that can be given BY THE FINGERS ALONE. Great caution, however, must be used in beginning this practice; for, if the force is obtained by stiffening the fingers and lifting the hand and arm, it will be worse than useless. Only so much power may be employed as is consistent with flexibility and suppleness; and in order to allow moderate accents to be heard in contrast with other tones, *all those that are unaccented must be soft.* Strength will gradually increase, and with it, power of tone. All the tones, whether accented or not, must also be *legato.* Learners are very likely, in playing rapidly, with occasional accents, to disconnect the tone preceding each accent, and to raise the hand and arm to increase the force. They are also liable to strike, with undue force, several tones in the vicinity of each accent.

THE PUPIL SHOULD COUNT DISTINCTLY; at first, with every tone, then with every accent only; and when the occasional accents are employed, with every rhythmic group; *the first count being always simultaneous with the first accent.* All the exercises upon scales, broken chords, and arpeggios must be thoroughly learned. Merely playing them over a few times with the aid of notes amounts to very little in advancing real musical education. When the pupil plays them before the teacher, to show the result of previous practice, the book should be closed; both teacher and pupil depending entirely upon the memory.

ACCENT EXERCISES UPON FIVE TONES.

Directions.—Practice, at first, with each hand separately. Make all the tones perfectly distinct, *legato,* and equal in time. Particular care is necessary that the tone which precedes each accent should be *legato.*

No. 56.

ACCENT OF FOURS.—Count four, one for each tone, and accent with finger and voice the first part of each measure.

No. 57.

ACCENT OF FOURS.—Count four, one for each group of sixteenth notes, and accent the first tone of each group.

Accent upon the first tone.   *Accent upon the second tone.*   *Accent upon the third tone.*

Accent upon the fourth tone.   *Accent upon the fifth tone.*

No. 58.

ACCENT OF EIGHTS.—Count four, one for each group of sixteenth notes. but omit the accent upon the second and fourth groups.

Accent upon the first tone.   *Accent upon the second tone.*   *Accent upon the third tone.*

Accent upon the fourth tone.   *Accent upon the fifth tone.*   *Accent upon the sixth tone.*

Accent upon the seventh tone.   *Accent upon the eighth tone.*

No. 59.

ACCENT OF SIXTEENS.—Count four, one for each group of sixteenth notes, but omit the accent upon the second, third and fourth groups. Place the accent also upon the other tones.

No. 60.

ACCENT OF TWELVES.—Count three, one for each group of sixteenth notes, and accent the first tone of the first group. Place the accent also upon the other tones.

No. 61.

ACCENT OF TWENTY-FOURS.—Count six, one for each group of sixteenth notes, and accent the first tone of the first group. Place the accent also upon the other tones.

No. 62.

ACCENT OF THREES.—Count three, one for each tone, and accent with voice and finger the first part of each measure. Begin the accentuation also upon the third, fourth, and fifth tones.

First accent upon the first tone.   First accent upon the second tone.

No. 63.

ACCENT OF THREES.—Count six, at first, one for each tone. Then, count two, one for each group of eighth notes, and accent the first tone of every group. The Left hand is to play an octave lower than the Right, reading from the same notes. Place the accent also upon the other tones.

RIGHT.

LEFT.

No. 64.

ACCENT OF SIXES.—Count two, one for every group of eighth notes, but omit the accent upon the second group. Accent also the other tones.

No. 65.

ACCENT OF NINES.—Count three, one for every group, and accent the first tone of the first group.

No. 66.

ACCENT OF TWELVES—Count four, one for each group of eighth notes, and accent the first tone of the first group. There should be a decided difference between this Accent of Twelves, which is composed of four groups of three tones each, and that of No. 60, which is formed of three groups of four tones each.   Besides the strong accent which is marked (≥) there should be a slight accent, sufficient to indicate the grouping to the ear, upon the first tone of every group.   Place the accent also upon the third tone.

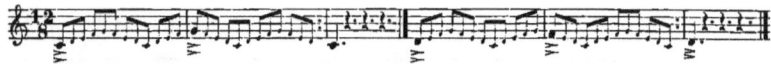

No. 67.

ACCENT OF EIGHTEENS.   *Triplets.*—Count six, one for every triplet of sixteenths, and accent the first tone in each measure.   Place the accent also upon the other tones.

No. 68.

ACCENT OF EIGHTEENS.   *Sextolets.*—Count three, one for every sextolet, and accent the first tone of each measure.

If it is difficult to do so without producing the effect of two triplets, thus : count nine, at first, as follows :

Place the accent also upon the other tones.

The principles of § 80 are still further illustrated in No. 69, which shows one of the many ways in which any five-finger exercise may be expanded, made interesting and much more useful, by accentual treatment.

COMMON FORMS.

Parallel Motion.

Contrary Motion.

No. 69.

Accent of Nines. *Parallel Motion.*— Count three.

Contrary Motion.

ACCENT EXERCISES UPON TWO TONES.

No. 70.

Accent of Fours.—Count four, one for each group of sixteenth notes, and accent the first tone of every group. Practice also with Accent of Eights, by omitting the accent upon the second and fourth groups in every measure, and with Accent of Sixteens, by omitting the accent upon the second, third, and fourth groups. Repeat many times.

Accent upon the lower tones.

RIGHT. ✗ 1 ✗ 1

LEFT.

Accent upon the higher tones.

Practice the following ACCENTS OF TWELVES, TWENTY-FOURS, THREES, &c., Nos. 71 to 79 inclusive, upon A and B, B and C, C and D, &c., like No. 70, to give all the fingers equal discipline.

No. 71.

ACCENT OF TWELVES.—Count three.

No. 72.

ACCENT OF TWENTY-FOURS.—Count six.

No. 73.

ACCENT OF THREES.—Count two, one for every group of eighth notes. Omit the accent upon the second group in each measure to produce ACCENT OF SIXES.

No. 74.

ACCENT OF NINES.—Count three.

No. 75.

ACCENT OF TWELVES.—Count four.

No. 76.

ACCENT OF EIGHTEENS. *Triplets.*—Count six.

No. 77.

ACCENT OF TWENTY-FOURS.—Count eight.

No. 78.

ACCENT OF EIGHTEENS. *Sextolets.*—Count three. (See No. 68.)

No. 79.

ACCENT OF TWENTY-FOURS.—Count four.

ACCENT EXERCISES UPON THREE TONES.

Accent of Fours.—Count one for each group.

No. 80.

Accent upon the first tone.

Accent upon the second tone.

Accent upon the third tone.

No. 81.

Accent of Eights.

No. 82.

Accent of Sixteens.

No. 83.

Accent of Twelves.

No. 84.

Accent of Twenty-fours.

Commence also with the other tones when applying accents of eights, twelves, sixteens and twenty-fours.

Accent of Threes.—Count one for each group.

No. 85.

No. 86.

Accent of Sixes.

No. 87.

Accent of Nines.

No. 88.

Accent of Twelves.

No. 89.

Accent of Eighteens.—Accent also other tones.

The following are the first measures of other three-toned exercises, to be completed by the pupil.

No. 90.

No. 91.

No. 92.

No. 93.

No. 94.

ACCENT EXERCISES UPON FOUR TONES.

No. 95.

ACCENT OF FOURS.

Accent upon the first tone.   *Upon the second tone.*   *Upon the third tone.*   *Upon the fourth tone.*

No. 96.   No. 97.

ACCENT OF TWELVES.   ACCENT OF TWENTY-FOURS.
Accent also the second, third, and fourth tones.

ACCENT OF THREES.   No. 98.

ACCENT OF SIXES.   No. 99.

ACCENT OF NINES.   No. 100.

ACCENT OF EIGHTEENS.   No. 101.

The following are the first measures of other four-toned exercises to be completed by the pupil.

No. 102.   No. 103.   No. 104.

ACCENT EXERCISES, WITH ONE KEY HELD BY EACH HAND.

No. 105.

Directions.—The keys to be held should, in every instance, be struck before the others, as indicated in the first measure, and be kept down while the accompanying sixteenths are many times repeated. All the exercises should be varied by accentuation ; the first is written eight times to illustrate this mode of playing them. Use the hands separately at first. Be sure to maintain flexibility, and to do precisely what should be done. Without very close watching, some keys that should be allowed to rise will be held, and others, that should be held, will come up. Move the fingers slowly. Rapidity, at first, entirely destroys the usefulness of this kind of exercises. It is not expedient to try to overcome the difficulties of all these exercises at once. A few moments of well directed practice every day will conquer them in time.

The foregoing Accent Exercises should now be transposed into various other keys. This, in some cases, will require both thumb and fifth finger to be placed upon black keys, and will bring other fingers into awkward positions. Figure 40 shows the points touched by thumb and fingers of a hand of medium size, when playing in the key of D♭. The hand of the pupil should be placed upon the paper, and made flat across the knuckle joints. Then, as the fingers are brought to the places indicated, the correct position for each one will be apparent.

Figure 40.

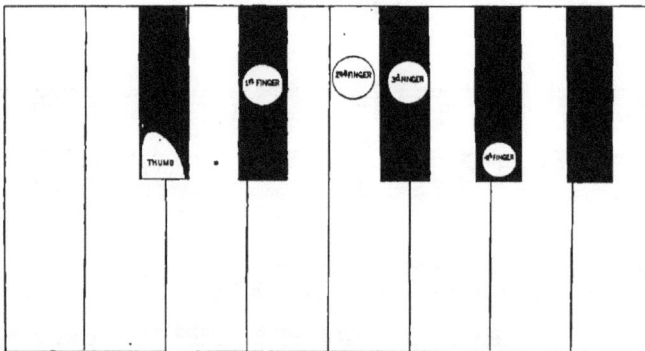

ACCENT EXERCISES UPON THE CHROMATIC SCALE.

Directions.—The following exercises should be practiced with both hands together, the Left playing an octave lower than the written notes. The fingering should everywhere conform to the principles of § 189, 1, p. 234, and the accentuation to those of § 80, p. 146. It will not be difficult to commit to memory the various exercises that are written in full and to supply the unwritten portions of the others. They should all be practiced to the end.

No. 106.

ACCENT OF FOURS.—Count three, and give the rests their full time. These passages commence with successive tones of the Diatonic Scale of C, ascend or descend au octave, and return.

No. 107.

ACCENT OF SIXES.—Count two, and play the following as written, with two sextolets in each measure, and also as if written with four triplets, thus :

This exercise differs from the preceding in accent only.

No. 108.

ACCENT OF FOURS.—In the first half of this exercise, each passage closes on the next key but one to the right of that with which it began ; the next passage commencing with the same key. In the last half of the exercise, each passage closes on the next key but one to the left ; the next passage commencing with the same key.

No. 109.

ACCENT OF SIXES.—This exercise differs from the preceding in accent only.

No. 110.

ACCENT OF FOURS.—A continuous exercise upon the plan of the preceding—the long tones and rests being omitted.

No. 111.

ACCENT OF SIXES.—This exercise differs from the preceding in accent only.

The artistic performance of a long and difficult composition can be attained by those only who possess or acquire the power of concentrating the entire force of the mind upon it, not only in single passages, but throughout the whole. Exercises which can not be played rapidly without great concentration are therefore of the highest value in the training of learners. Such are the following exercises upon the chromatic scale, and many of those upon the diatonic scale which ensue. They should be practiced, at first, slowly, to ensure accuracy, and then perseveringly, until they can be played very rapidly, with each accent clearly and distinctly given by both hands, and without a mistake. No one need be discouraged if many trials be unsuccessful.

No. 112.

ACCENT OF NINES.—This exercise differs from the preceding in accent and in length. It ascends to c three times. (See § 80, 3.)

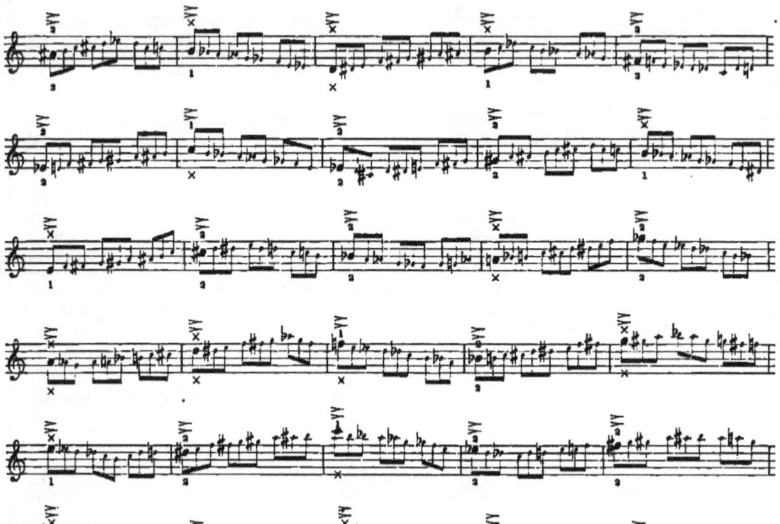

No. 113.

ACCENT OF NINES.—The following are the first two of a series of passages commencing upon successive tones of the diatonic scale of C; each requiring the hands to pass three times through the compass of one octave.

etc.

No. 114.

ACCENT OF SIXES.—In the first part of this exercise the hands play thirteen keys towards, and twelve keys from each other in every passage. In the last part, beginning with the twenty-second measure, they play twelve keys towards, and thirteen from each other. Play also with ACCENT OF FOURS.

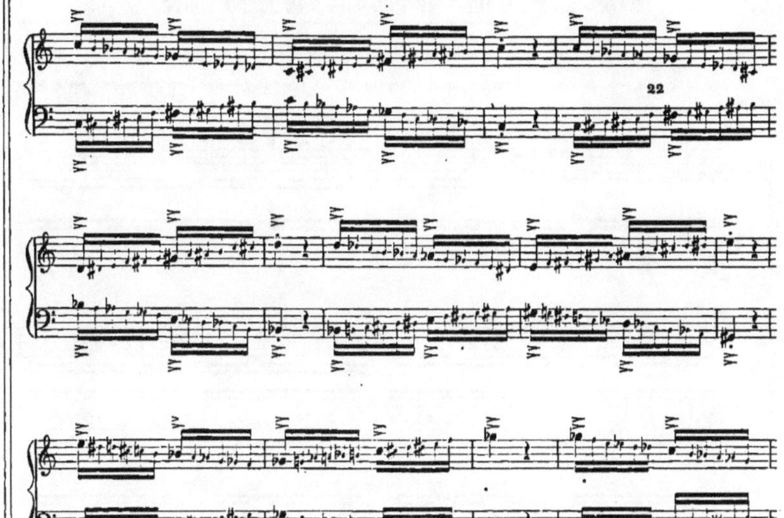
22

No. 115.

ACCENT OF FOURS.—A continuous exercise upon the plan of the preceding,—the long tones and rests being omitted.

No. 116.

ACCENT OF SIXES.— This exercise differs from the preceding in accent only.

No. 117.

ACCENT OF NINES.—This exercise is No. 112, arranged in contrary motion. (See page 161.)

ACCENT EXERCISES UPON DIATONIC SCALES.

Directions.—Before applying accentuation to the diatonic scales, the pupil should be very sure in regard to the fingering; otherwise the tendency to use the stronger fingers, where stress is needed, will constantly cause errors in their succession. It should be remembered that all scale passages, however the tones may be combined or arranged, if one only is played by each hand, are fingered like the simplest scale in the same key. (See § 25, p. 20, § 189, 2, p. 234.) Each mode of accenting should be practiced continuously up and down the scale until the accent falls again upon the same tone and part of the measure with which the exercise commenced. This, for some modes of accenting, will require many repetitions, as will be explained with the exercises; for this reason they are especially valuable, as they furnish a most excellent discipline for both the mind and fingers of the pupil. When they can be played rapidly, IN ALL THE KEYS, *without hesitation, without incorrect tones or fingering,* and with each accent clearly and roundly brought out, real and commendable proficiency in the Art of Playing the Piano-forte will have been made, and the pupil will have great reason for satisfaction. Remember that all the unaccented tones should be light and soft.

COMPASS OF ONE OCTAVE.   PARALLEL MOTION.

No. 118.

ACCENT OF FOURS.—Count four, and accent the first tone of each group. The hands ascend and descend eight times.

No. 119.

ACCENT OF EIGHTS.—This exercise is the same as the preceding, except that, in every measure, the accent is omitted upon the second and fourth groups.

No. 120.

ACCENT OF SIXTEENS.—This exercise also is the same as No. 118, except that, in every measure, the accent is omitted upon the second, third and fourth groups.

Close each of the following exercises with a short, crisp touch, and wait the exact time of the rests before repeating it.

No. 121.

ACCENT OF THREES.—Count two, accenting the first tone of every group. The hands ascend and descend three times.

No. 122.

ACCENT OF SIXES.—This exercise differs from the preceding only in the omission of the accent upon the second group in each measure.

No. 123.

ACCENT OF NINES. *Triplets.*—Count three, and omit the accent upon the second and third groups. The hands ascend and descend nine times.

COMPASS OF ONE OCTAVE. CONTRARY MOTION.

No. 124.

ACCENT OF THREES.

No. 125.

ACCENT OF SIXES.

Apply also the Accent of Fours, Eights, Nines, and Sixteens to the compass of one octave, contrary motion.

All the foregoing scales, Nos. 118 to 125 inclusive, may be varied by placing the first accent upon the second, third, fourth, or any other tone except the first.

COMPASS OF TWO OCTAVES.

No. 126.

ACCENT OF FOURS.—Count four, accenting the first tone of every group. The hands ascend and descend four times.

No. 127.

ACCENT OF EIGHTS.—This exercise is the same as No. 126, except that the accent is omitted upon the second and fourth groups.

No. 128.

ACCENT OF SIXTEENS.—This exercise also is the same as No. 126, except that the accent is omitted upon the second, third, and fourth groups.

No. 129.

ACCENT OF THREES.—In this exercise the measures consist of two groups of three tones each. Count two, and accent the first tone of each group. The hands ascend and descend three times.

No. 130.

ACCENT OF SIXES.—This exercise differs from No. 129 only in the omission of the accent upon the second group.

No. 131.

ACCENT OF NINES.—These measures consist of three groups. Count three, and omit the accent upon the second and third groups. The hands ascend and descend nine times.

Nos. 126 to 131, inclusive, should also be practiced in contrary motion, and with the accent upon other tones.

COMPASS OF THREE OCTAVES.   PARALLEL MOTION.

No. 132.

ACCENT OF THREES.—Count two. The hands ascend and descend once.

No. 133.

ACCENT OF SIXES.

No. 134.

ACCENT OF NINES.—Count three. The hands ascend and descend three times.

Very long and useful exercises may be produced by playing in 4–4 time, through the compass of three octaves, with ACCENT OF FOURS, EIGHTS, and SIXTEENS. The hands will ascend and descend eight times.

COMPASS OF FOUR OCTAVES. PARALLEL MOTION.

No. 135.

The following exercise, though printed without accents, should be accented by the learner, thus: with Accent of Fours, by accenting the first tone of each group; with Accent of Eights, by omitting, in every measure, the accent upon the second and fourth groups; and with Accent of Sixteens, by omitting it upon the second, third, and fourth groups. Count four. The hands ascend and descend twice.

In the following exercise, the measures consist of six groups of four tones each, and may be played with Accent of Fours, by accenting the first tone of each group; with Accent of Twelves, by omitting, in every measure, the accent upon the second, third, fifth, and sixth groups; and with Accent of Twenty-fours, by accenting only the first tone of each measure.

No. 136.

Accent of Twenty-fours. Count six. The hands ascend and descend three times.

COMPASS OF FOUR OCTAVES.   PARALLEL MOTION.

No. 137.

ACCENT OF NINES.   *Triplets.*—Count three.   The hands ascend and descend nine times.

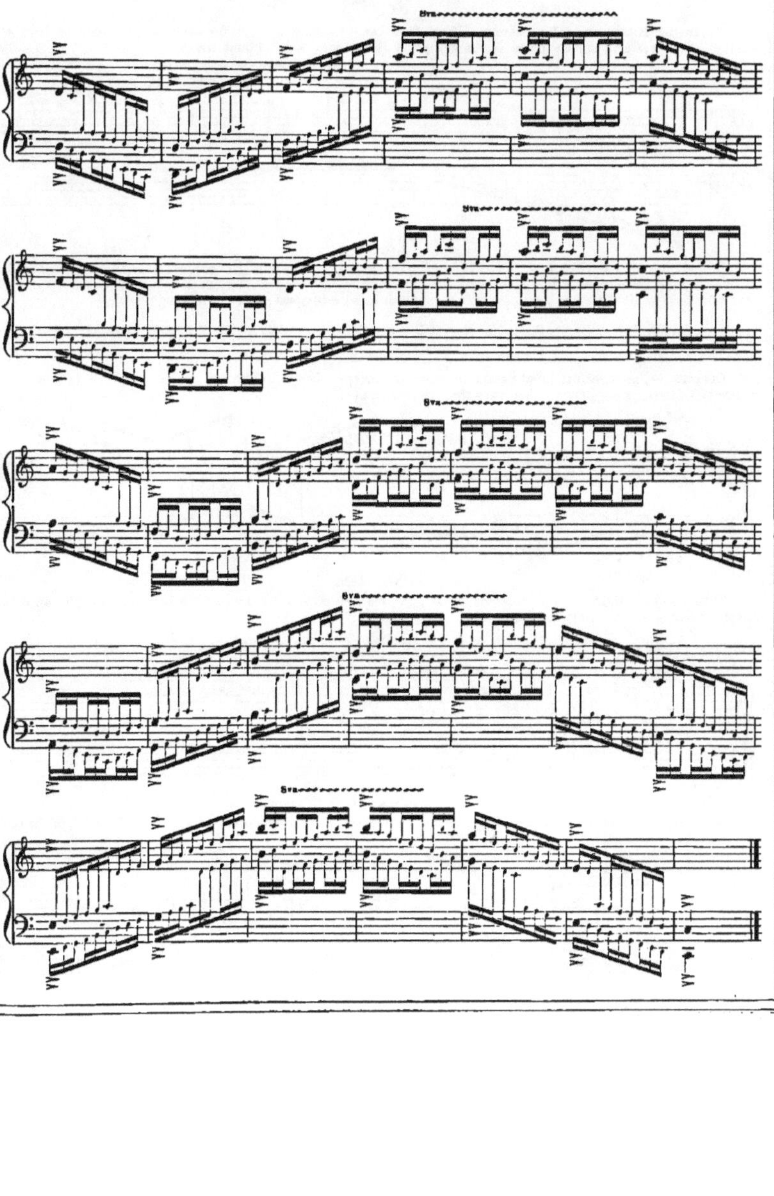
8va

No. 138.

ACCENT OF EIGHTEENS.—This exercise differs from the preceding only in the omission of alternate bars and accents. The measures are composed of six groups of three tones each. Count six.

In the following exercises, Nos. 139 to 146 inclusive, contrary and parallel motions, are constantly succeeding each other; the arrangement being dependent upon the fact that one hand may go through a certain compass,—say two or four octaves,—while the other hand plays through half as great a compass twice in the same time.

CONTRARY AND PARALLEL MOTIONS COMBINED.   OCTAVES, THIRDS AND SIXTHS.[1]

No. 139.

OCTAVES.—The Right hand first passes through two octaves; then twice through one octave. The Left hand first passes twice through one octave; then once through two octaves.

No. 140.

THIRDS.—The Right hand commences on III, and the Left on I, of the scale. The Left may also play an octave lower, producing tenths instead of thirds.

No. 141.

SIXTHS.—An inversion of the preceding exercise. The Right hand commences on I, and the Left on III, of the scale.

(1) See Chapter VII. Theoretical Department, p. 228.

No. 142.

ACCENT OF SIXTEENS. *Thirds.*—The Right hand first passes through four octaves; then twice through two octaves. The Left hand first passes twice through two octaves; then once through four octaves.

No. 143.

ACCENT OF SIXTEENS. *Sixths.*—An inversion of the preceding exercise.

No. 144.

ACCENT OF NINES.   *Octaves* — The Right hand first passes through four octaves; then twice through two octaves. The Left hand first passes twice through two octaves; then once through four octaves.   This use of the hands is repeated four and one half times before the accent returns to the starting point.

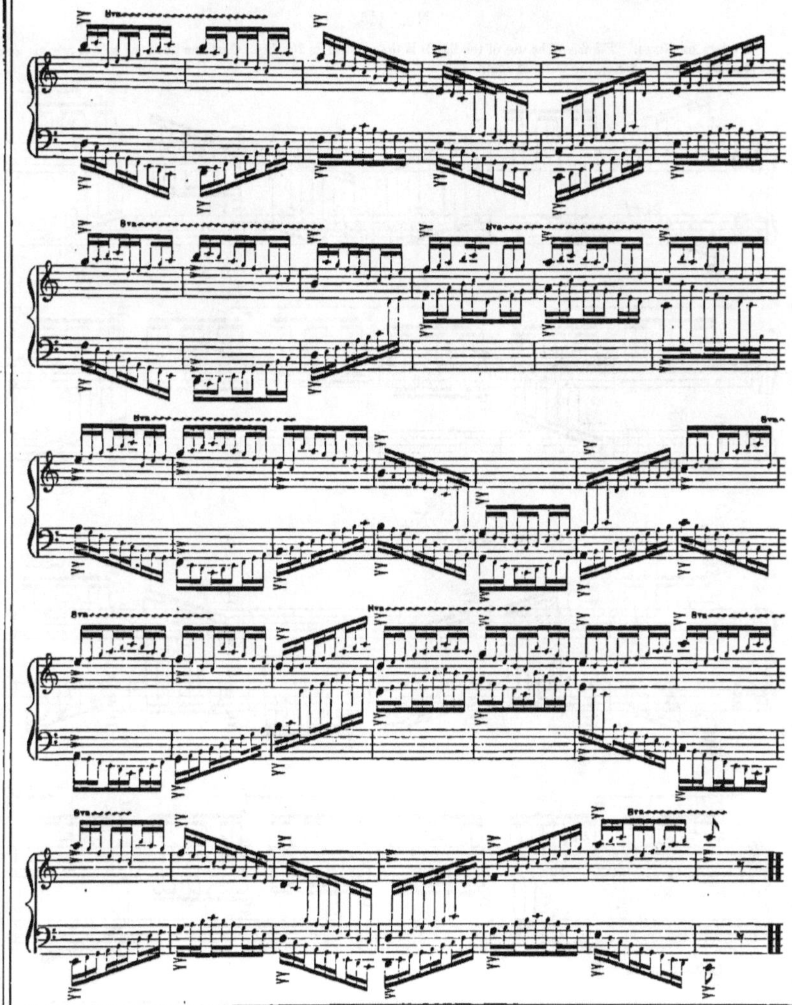

No. 145.

ACCENT OF NINES.   *Thirds.*—The use of the hands is the same as in No. 144. Continue until the accent returns to
the starting point, rendering the exercise complete.

No. 146.

SIXTHS.—Continue until the exercise is complete.

etc.

Nos. 147 to 152 inclusive, are complete canons, in which one part follows the other, in exact imitation, to the end. Nos. 147 to 150 inclusive, are preliminary, showing how a part played by one hand may ascend to a certain point and turn to descend, while that played by the other is still ascending, and *vice versa*. All the accents should be employed, though none are indicated with the notes.

No. 147.

No. 148.

No. 149.

No. 150.

No. 151.

The first ascent in this exercise is an octave; the second, a ninth; the third, a tenth; the fourth, an eleventh; and so on, until the compass of two octaves is reached. Then each ascent is less than the preceding, until the compass of one octave is regained, and the exercise is either repeated or closed. Each ascent is made from I, of the Scale.

No. 152.

In the first half of this exercise each ascent is an octave, and each descent a seventh. In the last half, each descent is an octave, and each ascent a seventh. (See Remark, page 161.)

EXERCISE No. 153.

Directions.—This exercise should be carried through two octaves, and practiced with all the fingers and a variety of accents. It has been highly recommended by LISZT, and others, as one of the best means of increasing the strength of the fingers. Practice it vigorously until the muscles are weary; then, after sufficient rest, repeat the effort. It may also be played in contrary motion.

ACCENT OF TWOS.

ACCENT OF FOURS.

Accent upon the first tone.   *Upon the second.*   *Upon the third.*   *Upon the fourth.*

ACCENT OF THREES.   ACCENT OF SIXES.   ACCENT OF NINES.

Practice in like manner with the following fingering.

All the accents may also be applied to this exercise when played *staccato*.

ACCENT EXERCISES UPON BROKEN TRIADS.

Directions.—The following exercises are very valuable and interesting. In order to derive the greatest benefit from them, they should be played from memory. In all *legato* passages of broken chords, the last tone played while the hand is in one position, should be connected with the first tone of the next position. This requires *contraction* and *extension*. (See § 35, p. 38, § 40, p. 45.) As soon as the first tone of a position is struck, the hand should extend so that each finger may be held over its proper key. Some of the rhythmic groups are identical with the positions of the hand, and others are not; as, for example:

COMPASS OF THREE OCTAVES AND A THIRD.

No. 154.

ACCENT OF FOURS.—Count four, one for every group of sixteenths. If it is difficult to do this, count, at first, one for each tone, and accent the first tone of each group. The highest and lowest tones are struck twice.

Accent upon the first tone.

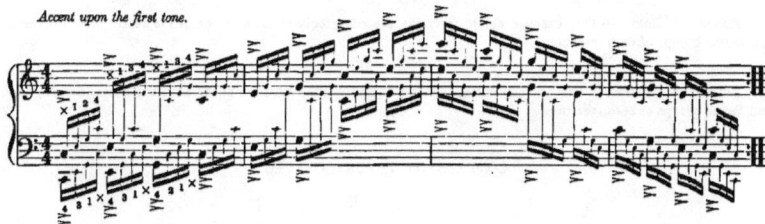

Accent upon the second tone. If this is counted one for each tone, it should begin thus: etc. The first ONE is always simultaneous with the first accent.

Accent upon the third tone.

Accent upon the fourth tone.

No. 155.

ACCENT OF EIGHTS.—This exercise differs from the preceding only in the omission of the accent upon the second and fourth groups of each measure.

No. 156.

ACCENT OF SIXTEENS.—This exercise differs from No. 154 only in the omission of the accent upon the second, third, and fourth groups of each measure.

COMPASS OF THREE OCTAVES.

No. 157.

ACCENT OF THREES.—Count two, one for every group of eighths, and accent the first tone of each group. If it is difficult to do this, count, at first, one for each tone. Accent on the first tone will commence thus: *One, two, three.*

Accent upon the second, thus: *three, One, two, three.* etc. Close each passage with a short, crisp touch, and wait the exact time of the rests before repeating it.

Accent upon the second tone.

Accent upon the third tone.

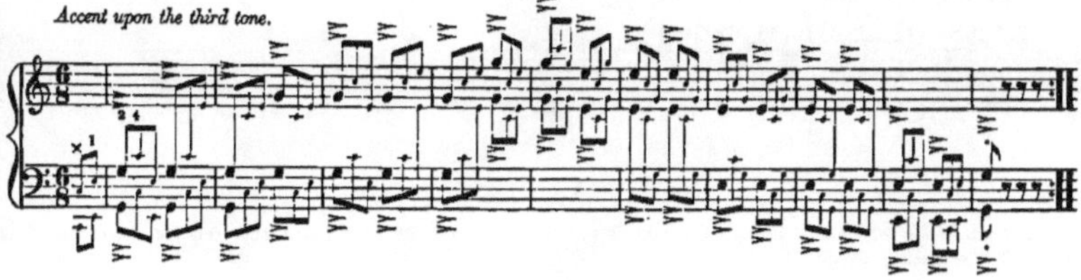

No. 158.

ACCENT OF SIXES.—This exercise differs from the preceding only in the omission of the accent upon the second group in each measure.

Accent upon the first tone.

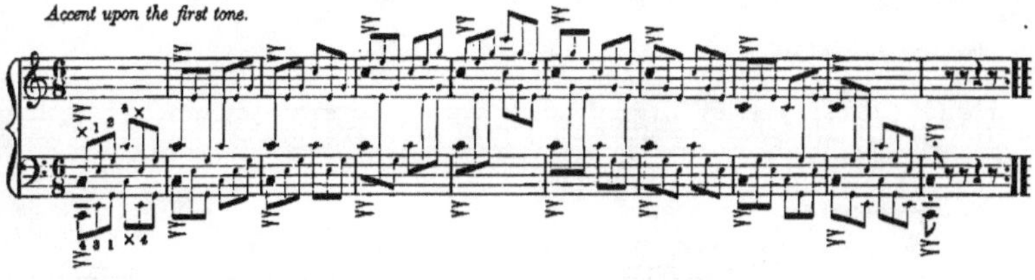

The Left hand is to play an octave lower than the Right in all the following exercises that are written upon one staff.

Accent upon the second tone.

Accent upon the third tone.

Accent upon the fourth tone.

Accent upon the fifth tone.

Accent upon the sixth tone.

No. 159.

ACCENT OF NINES.—Count three. Close each passage with a short crisp touch, and wait the exact time of the rests before repeating it.

Accent upon the first tone.

Accent upon the second tone.

Accent upon the third tone.

Accent upon the fourth tone.

Accent upon the fifth tone.

Accent upon the sixth tone.

Accent upon the seventh tone.

Accent upon the eighth tone.

Accent upon the ninth tone.

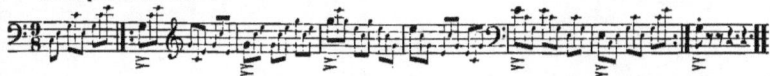

No. 160.

ACCENT OF TWELVES.—The measures are composed of four groups of three tones each.   Count four.

Nos. 154 to 160, inclusive, should now be varied by striking the tones as in the four following examples.   This, at first, will be somewhat perplexing.

No. 161.

ACCENT OF FOURS.—The order of the fingers is, either ✕, 2 or 3, 1, 4 ; or the reverse, 4, 1, 2 or 3, ✕.

No. 162.

The order of the fingers is, either ✕, 4, 1, 2 or 3 ; or the reverse, 4, ✕, 2 or 3, 1.

No. 163.

The order of the fingers is, either ✕, 2 or 3, 4, 1 ; or 4, 1, ✕, 2 or 3.

No. 164.

The order of the fingers is, either ✕, 1, 4, 2 or 3 ; or 4, 2 or 3, ✕, 1.

No. 165.

ACCENT OF SIXTEENS.—Practice this and the following exercise as rapidly as is consistent with perfect distinctness and a good position of the hand. Count four, omitting the accent upon the second, third and fourth groups of every measure.

No. 166.

ACCENT OF EIGHTEENS.—The following measures are composed of six groups of three tones each. Count six, omitting the accents upon all groups except the first.

The foregoing exercises upon Broken Triads are all written in the key of C. They should now be transposed. The TRIAD OF I, in each of the remaining Major keys, is indicated in the following table. All these chords should be fingered upon the same principles, and should receive the same accentual treatment as the chord of C. (See Chap. XIV, Theoretical Department, p. 231.)

TABLE.

Fifths	D	A	E	B	F#	C#	G#	C	F	Bb	Eb	Ab	Db	Gb
Thirds	B	F#	C#	G#	D#	A#	E#	A	D	G	C	F	Bb	Eb
Roots, which are also key-tones	G	D	A	E	B	F#	C#	F	Bb	Eb	Ab	Db	Gb	Cb
Signatures	One sharp	Two sharps	Three sharps	Four sharps	Five sharps	Six sharps	Seven sharps	One flat	Two flats	Three flats	Four flats	Five flats	Six flats	Seven flats

§ 82. *The Thumb upon Black Keys.*—For playing running passages legato, the thumb is certainly better adapted to the white keys than the black. In the old methods and schools of playing, this fact being over-estimated, the black keys were too carefully avoided. Now, however, the thumb is used more freely, and is trained to play black keys whenever real convenience requires it. The Triads of D and Eb, broken, for example, should be fingered thus :

MINOR TRIADS.

THE TRIAD OF I, in each of the Minor keys, is indicated by the following table. All these chords should be treated like the Major Triads upon the same roots.

TABLE.

Fifths	G	D	A	E	B	F#	C#	G#	D#	A#	F	C
Thirds	Eb	Bb	F	C	G	D	A	E	B	F#	Db	Ab
Roots, which are also key-tones	C	G	D	A	E	B	F#	C#	G#	D#	Bb	F
Signatures	Three flats	Two flats	One flat	Natural	One sharp	Two sharps	Three sharps	Four sharps	Five sharps	Six sharps	Five flats	Four flats

§ 83. *Chords of the Dominant Seventh.* —(§ 179, 1, p. 232.) Each of these chords has four positions, which are fingered as follows :

KEY OF C, MAJOR AND MINOR.   COMPONENT TONES OF THE CHORD, G, B, D, F.

The component tones of the other dominants are shown in the following

TABLE.

Sevenths....	C .	G	D	A	E	B	F♯	B♭	E♭	A♭	D♭	G♭	C♭	F♭
Fifths........	A	E	B	F♯	C♯	G♯	D♯	G	C	F	B♭	E♭	A♭	D♭
Thirds.......	F♯	C♯	G♯	D♯	A♯	E♯	B♯	E	A	D	G	C	F	B♭
Roots.	D	A	E	B	F♯	C♯	G♯	C	F	B♭	E♭	A♭	D♭	G♭
Signatures..	One sharp	Two sharps	Three sharps	Four sharps	Five sharps	Six sharps	Seven sharps	One flat	Two flats	Three flats	Four flats	Five flats	Six flats	Seven flats

ACCENT EXERCISES.

Directions.—The remarks and directions preceding Exercise No. 154, p. 185, are applicable also to these exercises. All the modes of accenting should be practiced in *all keys.*

No. 167.

ACCENT OF FOURS.   *Compass of Two Octaves and a Fifth.*

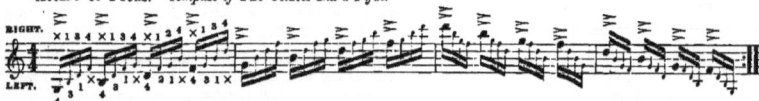

No. 168.

ACCENT OF THREES.   *Compass of Two Octaves and a Third.*

Position of the hand. Position. Position. Position.

§ 84. *Chords of the Diminished Seventh.*—(§ 179, 2, p. 232.)Each of these chords has four positions, which are fingered alike because the keys producing them are equidistant : two keys are omitted between the thumb and first finger, two between the first and third fingers, and two between the third and fourth. The component tones of the diminished sevenths are as follows :

FIRST CHORD.	SECOND CHORD.	THIRD CHORD.
G♯, B. D, F.	F♯, A, C, E♭.	C♯, E, G, B♭.
B♮, D, F, A♭.	A♮, C, E♭, G♭.	E♭, G, B♭, D♭.
D♮, F, A♭, C♭.	B♮, D♯, F♯, A.	F♯, A♯, C♯, E.
E♯, G♯, B, D.	D♮, F♯, A, C.	A♮, C♯, E, G.

ACCENT EXERCISES.

Directions.—The remarks and directions preceding Exercise No. 154, p. 185, are applicable also to this exercise. All the modes of accenting should be practiced in each chord.

No. 169.

FIRST CHORD. ACCENT OF FOURS. *Compass of Two Octaves and a Fifth.*

No. 170.

ACCENT OF THREES. *Two Octaves and a Third.*

The following exercise, consisting of successions of Diminished Sevenths, is very useful in training the hands to play freely among the black keys.

No. 171.

ACCENT OF FOURS. *Compass of two Octaves.*

No. 172.

ACCENT OF THREES.

Apply also ACCENT OF SIXES and NINES to this exercise.

ACCENT EXERCISES UPON ARPEGGIOS FORMED FROM TRIADS.

Directions.—In the following, the change from one hand to the other should be made so skillfully that no one can discover, *by ear*, where it occurs or which hand is used. All the tones should be perfectly *legato*. (See § 55, p. 62.)

No. 173.
KEY OF C MAJOR.   TRIAD OF I.

ACCENT OF FOURS.—Six groups in the measure. Count six, and speak the first ONE simultaneously with the first accent.

Practice the above arpeggios with different accentuation, and also transpose them into all the other Major keys. In the keys of G, D, A, E, B, F♯, and F, the fingering will be the same as in C. The second finger may be used by small hands.

In the key of B♭ the thumb may be placed upon either D or F. In the keys of E♭, A♭, and D♭, the thumb should be upon the only white key in each chord.

ARPEGGIOS OF VARIOUS CHORDS.

§ 85. Particular attention is requested to the following exercises, in which various Arpeggios are produced mechanically by a few simple changes of the fingers. They include a variety of effects resulting from harmonic and accentual modifications, which are very pleasing to the ear and entirely exclude monotony. They also afford valuable aid in equalizing the touch and increasing the power of the fingers. These arpeggio passages are so common in modern music—one or more of them occurring in almost every composition for the Piano-forte,—that it is highly important for every learner to acquire complete command of them.

The chord of the Diminished Seventh in the following position : being the basis upon which the various changes are made, will, for convenience, be called the *Primary position.* An Arpeggio formed from this chord is played by the Left hand alone through the compass of four octaves ascending, and by the Right hand alone through the same compass descending. When this arpeggio becomes somewhat familiar, harmonic changes are introduced. Accentuation is employed in accordance with the principles explained in § 80, p. 146.

All the modes of accenting these exercises must be diligently practiced, though they are not written in full. The notes that are given are only hints to aid the memory at first. The following measures are composed of four groups of four tones each.

No. 174.

ACCENT OF FOURS.—Count four. Accent with each counting.

Accent upon the first tone.

Accent upon the second tone.

Accent upon the third tone.

Accent upon the fourth tone.

No. 175.

ACCENT OF EIGHTS.—Omit the accent upon the second and fourth groups. Place the accent upon all the other tones.

Accent upon the first tone.

Accent upon the second tone.

No. 176.

ACCENT OF SIXTEENS.—Omit the accent upon the second, third, and fourth groups.

Accent upon the first tone.

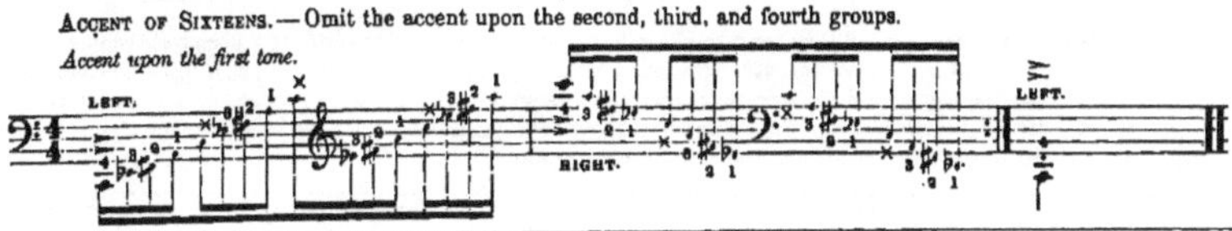

Accent upon the second tone.

LEFT HAND.

RIGHT.

LEFT.

Each of the other fourteen tones should, in turn, receive accent, and thus become the first tone of a measure ; the first accent and first counting being always simultaneous. The following example, by way of further illustration, shows this exercise so written as to bring the

Accent upon the tenth tone.

LEFT.

RIGHT.

LEFT.

No. 177.

ACCENT OF THREES.—The following measures are composed of four groups of three tones each. Count three, and accent the first tone of every group. Apply also ACCENT OF SIXES, which is produced by omitting the accent upon the second and fourth groups of each measure.

LEFT.

RIGHT.

LEFT.

RIGHT.

LEFT.

RIGHT.

LEFT.

No. 178.

ACCENT OF NINES produces a very long exercise commencing as follows. Count three. (§ 80, 3, p. 146.) ACCENT OF EIGHTEENS is produced by omitting alternate bars and accents. (See No. 67, p. 150.)

LEFT.

RIGHT.

LEFT.

&c.

Changes of Harmony.—All the chords resulting from the changes here described should be practiced thoroughly as Arpeggios, and treated in the same manner, in regard to accent, as the primary chord. Finally, when they are quite familiar, they should be played in quick succession, each chord ascending and descending once ; and also, the first chord ascending, the second descending, the third ascending, the fourth descending, and so on, with accents of sixteen and eighteen, until the utmost freedom, facility, and rapidity are attained.

No. 180.

FIRST HARMONIC CHANGE.—Placing the Left hand in the *primary position*, spoken of in § 85, and moving the first finger one key to the left, the chord produced will be A♭, C, E♭, and F♯. As this chord is played by the same keys as the dominant seventh chord in the key of D♭, it will appear more familiar written with G♭ instead of F♯.

No. 181.

SECOND HARMONIC CHANGE.—Returning again to the primary position, and moving the second finger one key to the left, the chord produced will be as follows:

No. 182.

THIRD HARMONIC CHANGE.—Returning to the primary position, and moving the third finger to the left, produces the following chord:

Before making each change, the hand must return to the primary position.

No. 183.

FOURTH CHANGE.—The first and second fingers are moved to the left.

No. 184.

FIFTH CHANGE.—The second and third fingers are moved to the left.

No. 185.

SIXTH CHANGE.—The first, second and third fingers are moved to the left.

No. 186.

SEVENTH CHANGE.—The thumb and fourth finger are moved to the left. This is the dominant seventh chord in the key of E, and should be written as follows:

The Left hand must return to the Primary position before each change. (*See* § 85, p. 194.)

No. 187.

EIGHTH CHANGE.—The first finger is moved one key to the right.

RIGHT.

LEFT HAND.   LEFT.

No. 188.

NINTH CHANGE.—The second finger is moved the right.

RIGHT.

LEFT.   LEFT.

No. 189.

TENTH CHANGE.—The third finger is moved to the right.

RIGHT.

LEFT.   LEFT.

No. 190.

ELEVENTH CHANGE.—The first and second fingers are moved to the right.

No. 191.

TWELFTH CHANGE.—The second and third fingers are moved to the right.

No. 192.

THIRTEENTH CHANGE.—The first, second and third fingers are moved to the right.

No. 193.

FOURTEENTH CHANGE.—The thumb and fourth finger are moved to the right.

Nos. 194 and 195 are continuous exercises upon the primary chord and three harmonic changes.

No. 194.

PRIMARY CHORD.

FIRST HARMONIC CHANGE.

SECOND HARMONIC CHANGE.

THIRD HARMONIC CHANGE.

No. 195.

PRIMARY CHORD.

EIGHTH HARMONIC CHANGE.

NINTH HARMONIC CHANGE.

TENTH HARMONIC CHANGE.

A continuous exercise upon the primary chord and twelve harmonic changes—all except those in which the thumb moves,—should now be practiced until difficulties are overcome, the hands are fully accustomed to such passages, and great skill, facility and rapidity in playing them are attained. Exercises 174 to 195, inclusive, should also be practiced by the Right hand ascending, and the Left descending. These motions are more difficult than the reverse, already given. The hands should be turned in the manner described in § 55, and the tones carefully connected.

No. 196.

PRIMARY CHORD of § 85, for both hands, in Sixths.—ACCENT OF FOURS.—Count four.

Accent upon the first tone.

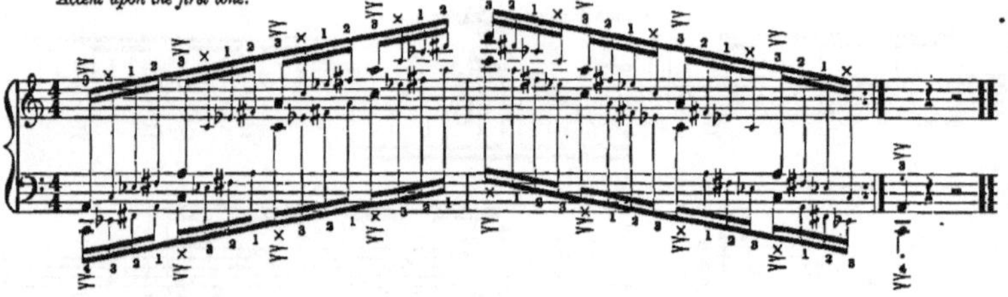

Accent upon the second tone.

Accent upon the third tone.

Accent upon the fourth tone.

No. 197.

ACCENT OF EIGHTS.—This exercise differs from No. 196 only in the omission of the accent upon the second and fourth groups in each measure. It is, however, susceptible of four more varieties produced by placing the accent upon the fifth, sixth, seventh and eighth tones, and it is quite essential that all of them should be very thoroughly practiced.

Accent upon the first tone.

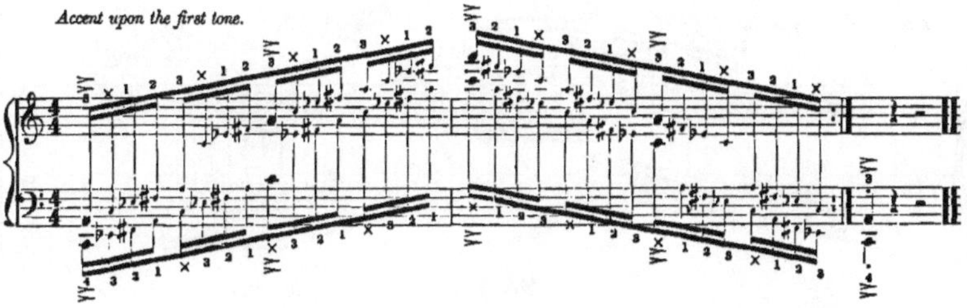

Accent upon the fifth tone.

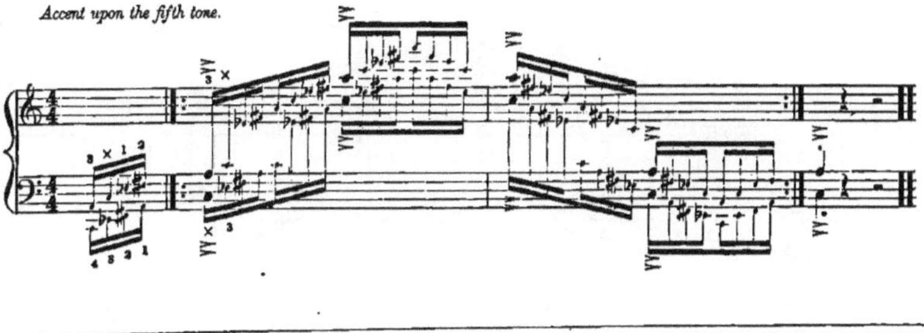

Accent upon the sixth tone.

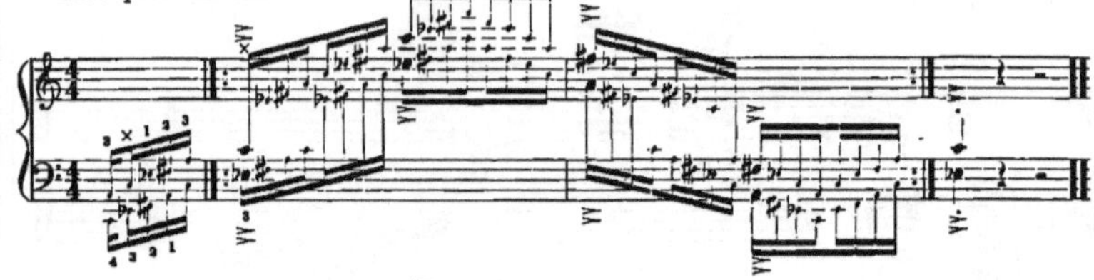

Accent upon the seventh tone.

Accent upon the eighth tone.

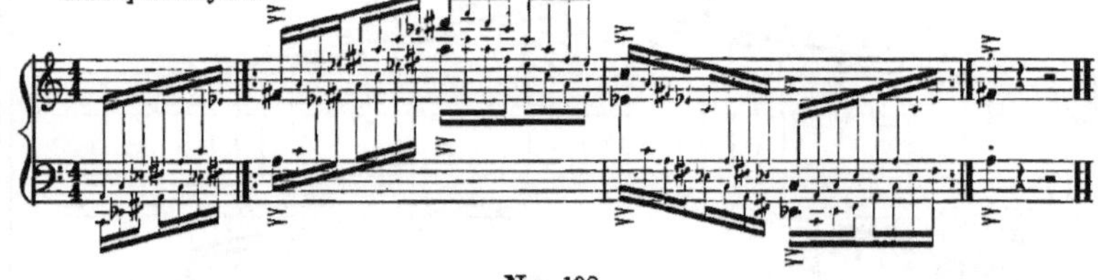

No. 198.

ACCENT OF SIXTEENS.—This exercise differs from No. 196 only in the omission of the accent upon the second, third and fourth groups in every measure. It is susceptible of sixteen varieties, produced by placing the accent upon each of the tones in turn, and all of them are very important.

Accent upon the first tone.

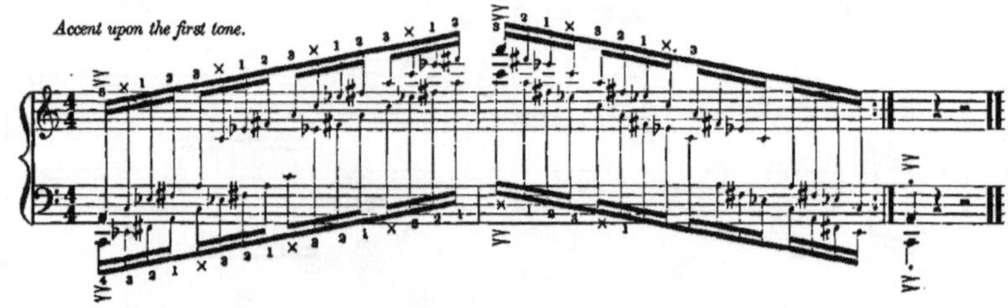

For accent upon the second, third, fourth, fifth, sixth, seventh and eighth tones, see Nos. 196 and 197. The following examples illustrate still further.

Accent upon the ninth tone.

Accent upon the tenth tone.

Accent upon the eleventh tone.

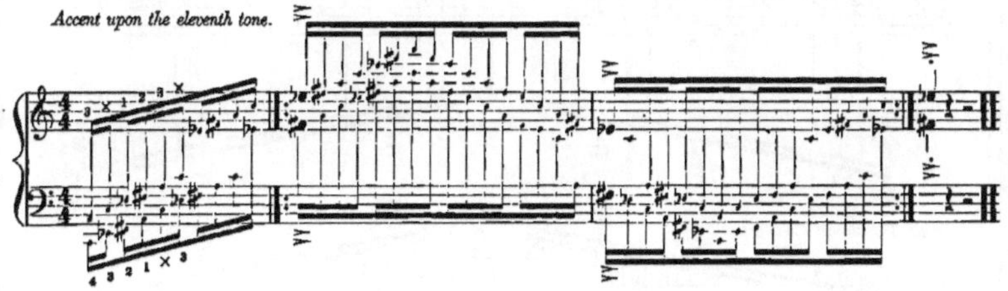

Accent upon the twelfth tone.

Accent upon the sixteenth tone.

No. 199.

FIRST HARMONIC CHANGE.

SECOND HARMONIC CHANGE.

THIRD HARMONIC CHANGE.

Each of the above arpeggios, and the other harmonic changes, described on pages 197 and 198, should receive the same accentual treatment as the primary chord.

No. 200.

ACCENT OF SIXTEENS.—The harmonic changes explained upon pages 197 and 198 should now be practiced in continuous exercises for both hands, of which the following is an example.

No. 201.

The other Diminished Seventh Chords may be taken as *primary chords*, and receive the same treatment, accentual and harmonic, which has been given to the first one, as, for example:

Primary Chord.   First harmonic change.   Second harmonic change.   Third harmonic change.

No. 202.

Primary Chord.   First change.   Second change.   Third change.

MODULATORY ARPEGGIOS.

§ 86. The harmonic changes of the following exercises may be explained mechanically thus: In the first measure, the Right hand is fitted to the first position of the triad of C: In the second, the middle parts are moved, the lower one key, black or white, and the upper two keys to the right, the third finger being substituted for the second: In the third measure, the upper of the middle parts is moved one key to the left, and taken by the second finger: In the fourth, the first finger is moved one key to the right: The fifth measure is a transposition of the first, each finger being moved one key to the right; the sixth is a transposition of the second; the ninth is another transposition of the first, each finger being moved two keys to the right; the tenth is another transposition of the second, and so on. In this way the exercise may be continued until all the Major keys are played in turn, and the triad of C recurs an octave above that in the first measure. When the circle of the keys can be played easily, accentuation should be applied.

The peculiarity of the arpeggios in No. 203 is, that the first and fourth fingers strike together.

No. 203.

Accent upon the first tone.

Accent upon the second tone.

Accent upon the third tone.

Accent upon the fourth tone.

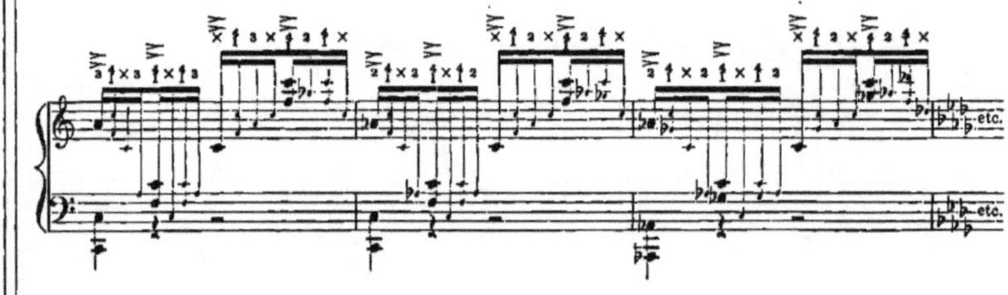

Accent upon the fifth tone.

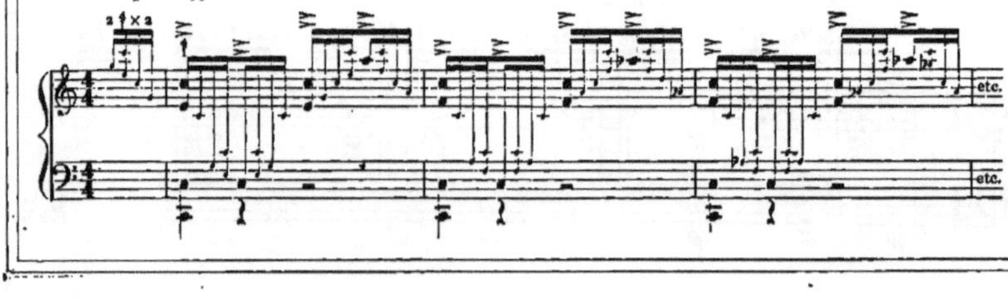

The peculiarity of the arpeggios in Nos. 204 and 205 is that the tones, and consequently the fingers, succeed each other in unusual order. In No. 204, the order in descending is, 2 4 1 ✕ or 3 4 1 ✕, and in ascending it is, ✕ 1 4 2 or ✕ 1 4 3. In No. 205, the order in descending is, 1 4 2 ✕ or 1 4 3 ✕, and in ascending it is, ✕ 2 4 1 or ✕ 3 4 1. Great care is needed in connecting the tones played by the first finger and thumb. The harmony in these arpeggios is identical with that of No. 203. Though no accents are given, all modes of practicing should be employed.

No. 204.

No. 205.

§ 87. *Broken Thirds.*—When the fingering of the double third scales has become familiar, they should be practiced in contrary motion, and also broken, as shown in the following exercises. Each scale is fingered in the same manner when broken, as when the tones are heard together. Broken third practice is very valuable for the hand. (See page 103 and § 189, 3, p. 234.)

SCALE OF C, IN DOUBLE THIRDS, BROKEN.

No. 206.

Accent of Fours.

Accent upon the first tone.

Accent upon the second tone.

No. 207.

Accent of Threes.

Accent upon the first tone.

Accent upon the second tone.

No. 208.

Accent of Nines.

Accent upon the first tone.

Accent upon the second tone.

§ 88. *Broken Sixths.*—When the fingering of the double sixth scales has become familiar, they should be practiced in contrary motion, and also broken, as shown in the following exercises. Each scale is fingered in the same manner when broken, as when the tones are struck together.

SCALE OF C, IN DOUBLE SIXTHS.   BROKEN.

No. 209.

Accent of Fours.—*Accent upon the first tone.*

No. 210.

Accent of Threes; or Sixes, by omitting alternate accents.
Accent upon the first tone.

No. 211.

Accent of Nines.

No. 212.

EXERCISE IN EXTENSION AND CONTRACTION. (See §§ 37, p. 42, and 40, p. 45.)

ACCENT EXERCISES UPON CHROMATIC OCTAVES.

THE RIGHT HAND ALTERNATING WITH THE LEFT.

When playing rapidly in this manner, the hands are guided by the eye, which watches the Left hand alone. (See Ex. 37, page 87.)   The following exercises are so written as to give all the accentuation to the Left hand.   By placing the first accent upon D♭, all may be given to the Right hand.

No. 213.

ACCENT OF FOURS.—Octaves with the Left hand, and single tones with the Right.

ACCENT OF SIXES.

No. 214.

ACCENT OF EIGHTS.

No. 215.

ACCENT OF TWELVES.

No. 216.

No. 217.

ACCENT OF FOURS.—Octaves with the Right hand, and single tones with the Left.

ACCENT OF SIXES.

No. 218.

ACCENT OF TWELVES.

No. 219.

ACCENT OF FOURS.—Octaves with both hands.

No. 220.

ACCENT OF SIXES.

No. 221.

ACCENT OF TWELVES.

No. 222.

ACCENT EXERCISES IN DOUBLE OCTAVES.

Directions. — The Exercises upon the Chromatic Scale, Nos. 106 to 117, inclusive, should now be practiced in Double Octaves. The fingering is, thumb and fourth finger for white keys, and thumb and third for black, thus :

The Diatonic Scales also may be treated in a similar manner. The following short exercises should be transposed, and afterward many of scales succeeding No. 118 should be practiced in octaves in different keys, until great facility, freedom and rapidity are attained.

No. 223.   No. 224.   No. 225.

ACCENT EXERCISES IN BROKEN OCTAVES.

Directions. — In practicing these exercises effort should be made, in every instance, to span the interval correctly the first time it is tried, that the hand, becoming accustomed to the extension required, may be able to strike an octave instantly and with perfect certainty. The Left hand should play an octave lower than the Right. Transpose.

No. 226.   No. 227.

No. 228.

TRILL EXERCISE.
No. 229.

Directions.—The following exercise is a very useful one if correctly practiced. The most important thing is strict time. Count four, and be sure that the movement is perfectly uniform throughout. The tendency will be to count too rapidly in the first measures, and too slowly in the eighth and ninth. Practice with all the fingers, thus:

```
RIGHT. X 1   X 2   1 2   1 3   2 3   2 4   3 4                      RIGHT. 1 X   2 X   2 1
       C D,  C D,  C D,  C D,  C D,  C D,  C D,  or the reverse, thus:   D C,  D C,  D C, &c.
LEFT.  1 X   2 X   2 1   3 1   3 2   4 2   4 3                      LEFT.  X 1   X 2   1 2
```

Accent upon the lower tone.

Accent upon the higher tone.

Use also the following tones to give varied discipline to the fingers. At (*A*) they are required to play a black key at the right of a white one; at (*B*) a black at the left of a white; at (*C*) two black keys; at (*D*) two white ones; at (*E*) a black, a minor third above a white, &c.

ACCENT STUDIES.

Directions.—The first *Etude* in Cramer's celebrated "STUDIO PER IL" is so universally known and esteemed as a superior exercise for training the hands that it has been selected for this work as a final illustration of the principles of § 80, p. 146. It is written in four different forms, the place of the accent being changed each time, thus varying the difficulty as well as the effect of the whole exercise, and giving a most thorough and valuable discipline to mind and fingers. The changes of accent involve a few slight modifications of the text in the first, ninth, tenth, nineteenth, twentieth, and twenty-first measures. The notation is made to conform to the principles explained in § 73, p. 86.

After the First Form can be played correctly it is most valuable practice to try and produce the other forms while reading from the same notes.

First Form.

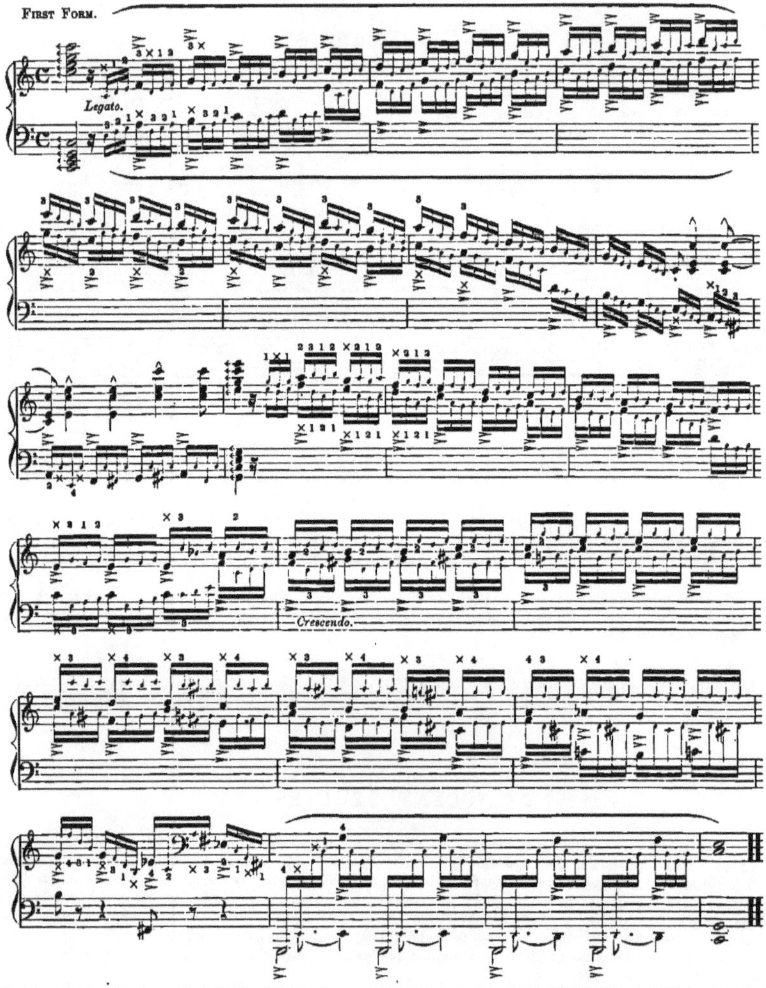

SECOND FORM.

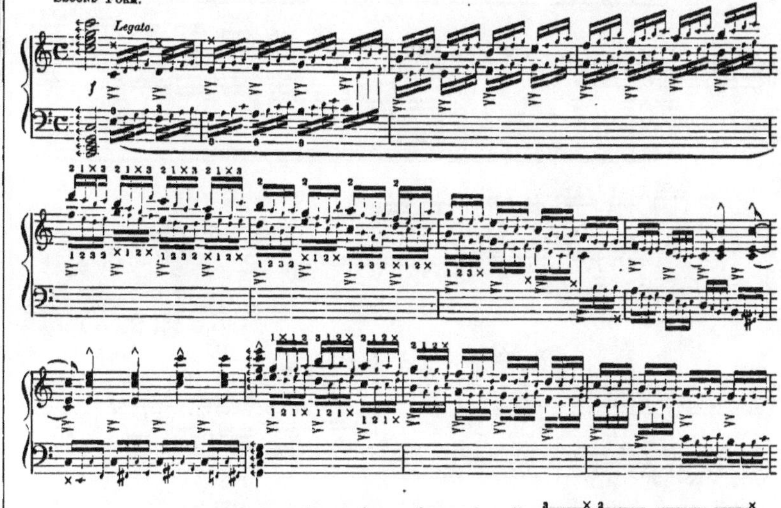

THIRD FORM.

Legato.

Fourth Form.

Legato.

IMPROVISATION.

§ 89. The playing of extemporaneous passages upon the Piano-forte is one of the most delightful ways of using the instrument. Complicated passages, composed in the highest style of the art, cannot, of course, be produced without great natural talent, aided by a mastery of Harmony and Counterpoint; but so much only of the science of harmony as is contained in Chapter XV, Theo. Dep., p. 232, coupled with some knowledge of melodic development, is sufficient, when made practically familiar, to enable an ordinary person to improvise easily a great number of simple, correct, and pleasing passages. Practical knowledge of harmony can be attained only by systematic study of chords and progressions, perseveringly continued until the mind is as familiar with them as with the words and phrases of common language, and they can be played with the utmost readiness. The following series of exercises are therefore proposed for those pupils who desire to enjoy the pleasure of improvisation.

§ 90. FIRST SERIES OF EXERCISES.—*Directions :* Transpose in writing the examples of § 181, then practice some of them daily without notes until all the chords in all keys are familiar, and every difficulty vanishes. Great assistance, at first, may be derived from stating aloud the name and scale-relationship of each chord as it is played: No. 3, § 181, for example, when played in the key of D, would be described thus : Triad of D Major, I in D Major. Triad of G Major, IV, in D Major. Triad of A Major, V, in D Major, &c.[1]

§ 91. SECOND SERIES OF EXERCISES.—*Directions :* Write all the Dominant and Diminished Seventh Chords, with all their positions and resolutions, in the same manner that those belonging to C, Major and Minor, are written in § 184. Then, by daily practice, attain a complete mastery of them.

§ 92. THIRD SERIES OF EXERCISES.— *Directions :* That faulty progressions may be avoided, first attempts at improvising should conform to the principles explained in § 182. But more freedom of movement will soon be demanded. The following scale-harmony illustrates how chords may be well connected without strict adherence to those principles. Transpose and practice until all keys are equally familiar. Name all the chords at first.

KEY OF C.   SCALE HARMONIZED.

§ 93. FOURTH SERIES OF EXERCISES.—*Directions :* All the chords known to the pupil may now be employed in MODULATION—which may be defined as any agreeable manner of conducting a succession of chords from one key to another. A few illustrations only can be given here. To make them valuable, they must first be fully understood, and then practiced until they can be used at any time, either in writing or upon the key-board, beginning in any key, without the possibility of being puzzled or lost. No. 1 is complete. Nos. 2, 3, and the last modulation of No. 4, should be carried out in a similar manner.

(1) Some may prefer the following names, which are employed in many works on Harmony; viz.: I is called the Tonic; II, the Supertonic; III, the Mediant; IV, the Sub-dominant; V, the Dominant; VI, the Sub-mediant; VII, the Leading-note. Then, instead of naming the chords as above, the pupil would say: Triad of D major, Tonic in D major, etc.

1. Modulation effected by treating the same chord as belonging, first, to that key in which it is the Triad of I, and second to that key in which it is the Triad of V.

No. 1.

Triad of I in the key of C. ⋯ Triad of V in the key of F. ⋯ Triad of I in F. ⋯ Triad of V in E♭. ⋯ Triad of I in E♭. ⋯ Triad of V in B♭. ⋯ Triad of I in B♭. ⋯ Triad of V in A♭. ⋯ Triad of I in A♭. ⋯ Triad of V in D♭. ⋯ Triad of I in D♭. ⋯ Triad of V in G♭. ⋯ Triad of I in G♭. ⋯ Triad of V in B. ⋯ Triad of I in B. ⋯ Triad of V in E. ⋯ Triad of I in E. ⋯ Triad of V in A. ⋯ Triad of I in A. ⋯ Triad of V in D. ⋯ Triad of I in D. ⋯ Triad of V in G. ⋯ Triad of I in G. ⋯ Triad of V in C. ⋯ Triad of I in C. ⋯

2. Modulation effected by treating the same chord, first, as the Triad of I, and second as the Triad of IV, in a new key.

No. 2.

Triad of I in C. ⋯ Triad of IV in G. ⋯ Triad of V in G. ⋯ Triad of I in G. ⋯ Triad of IV in D. ⋯ Triad of V in D. ⋯ Triad of I in D. ⋯ Triad of IV in A. ⋯ Triad of V in A. ⋯

3. Any Dominant Seventh Chord that contains one note of the chord preceding it, may be employed to effect an abrupt modulation into its own key.

No. 3.

Triad of I in key of C. ⋯ Dom. Sev. Chd. in key of D♭. ⋯ Triad of I key of D♭. ⋯ Dom. Sev. in key of D. ⋯ Triad of I in D. ⋯ Dom. Sev. in E♭. ⋯ Triad of I in E♭. ⋯ Dom. Sev. in E. ⋯ Triad of I in E. ⋯

4. Any Dominant-Seventh Chord may be changed into any other Dominant-Seventh Chord that containes one of its notes.

No. 4.

Dom. Sev. in F.
Dom. Sev. in A.
Dom. Sev. in C♯.
Triad of I in C♯ Minor.
Dom. Sev. in F.
Dom. Sev. in C.
Dom. Sev. in G.
Triad of I in G Major.
Dom. Sev. in F.
Dom. Sev. in D.
Dom. Sev. in B.
Triad of I in B Minor.
Dom. Sev. in F.
Dom. Sev. in B♭.
Dom. Sev. in E♭.
Dom. Sev. in A♭.
Dom. Sev. in D♭.

5. A Dominant-Seventh Chord may be changed into a Diminished-Seventh Chord by moving the finger which plays its root one key, black or white, to the right,—in other words, by sharping its root. Each Diminished-Seventh Chord may be changed into one of four Dominants by moving either of the fingers one key to the left.

No. 5.

Dom. Sev. Chd. in C.
Dim. Sev. Chd. in A Minor.
Triad of I in A Minor.
Dim. Sev. in A Minor.
Dom. Sev. in C.
Dim. Sev. in A Minor.
Dom. Sev. in A.
Dim. Sev. in A Minor.
Dom. Sev. in F♯.
Dim. in C Minor.
Dom. Sev. in E♭.

Notice that in each of the above modulations and changes one note, at least, belongs to both the modulating chord and the chord preceding it, and that it is in the same part in both chords.

§ 94. THE CONSTRUCTION OF MELODIES.—A succession of tones so regulated and modulated as to please the ear is called a melody. Analysis divides a melody into phrases, and subdivides a phrase, until a very few tones only are found to express the leading ideas upon which the whole is constructed, or from which it is developed. A musical idea, thus expressed by a few tones, which may be variously employed in the construction of a melody, is called a MOTIVO.

This group of three notes, for example : 𝄞 represents a motivo. It may be repeated, forming a measure

like this : 𝄞 ; it may be transposed, not into another key, but to another place in the same key,

thus : 𝄞 , and may receive other transformations without losing its identity. Another

motivo is represented by the following two tones : 𝄞 . It also may be repeated and transposed or expanded, thus :

𝄞 or, reversed, thus : 𝄞 or, repeated reversed, and transposed, all at the same time, thus : 𝄞

On page 75 may be seen an illustration of some of the many ways in which an interesting composition may be constructed from these two *motivos*. In the first measure the first *motivo* is repeated. In the second measure the second *motivo* is introduced, and then reversed and transposed. The ninth and tenth measures are treated as an extended *motivo*, and transposed to form the eleventh and twelfth measures. The harmony of these measures being treated in the same manner, they produce what is called a SEQUENCE. The sixteenth measure is formed from the second *motivo* twice transposed and reversed.

It is beyond the scope of this work to treat fully the construction of melodies; but enough has been said to show that it is a very interesting and important subject for those who wish to compose or improvise.[1]

§ 95. INTERLUDES are short instrumental passages between the stanzas of vocal music. The great number of tunes in use, and the many hymns, expressing widely different sentiments, which are sung to each one of them, make it hardly possible that written interludes should, in all cases, be appropriate, or that, when they are exclusively used, incongruous and unpleasant effects should be wholly avoided. It is, therefore, very desirable that players should be able to compose, extemporaneously, interludes which express the spirit of the hymn and tune sung, and so give life and animation to the whole performance. A good way to secure appropriateness and unity is to construct interludes upon *motivos* from the tunes themselves. This is not invariably necessary; for sometimes a contrast is pleasant, but generally unity will give better satisfaction. A few interludes illustrative of this subject are subjoined. They should be carefully analyzed in regard to both their melodic and harmonic construction. The first one is adapted to the tune called "*The Shining Shore*." The melodic *motivos* are very plainly taken from the tune. The harmonies are as follows: A passage of tenths, during which the tonic, G, is sustained; the triad of V in G; triad of I in G; dominant seventh chord in C; triad of I in C, with D, F♯, G♯ and A, as passing notes; dominant seventh in G; triad of VI in G; chord of the seventh of II in the key of G—, composed of A, C, E, G; triad of I, fifth in the Base; dominant seventh; triad of I.

The second example is adapted to the tune *Boylston*. The *motivos* are taken from the tune. The harmonies are these: Three positions of the triad of C, major; the dominant seventh chord in F; triad of I in F; triad of V in F; treated as triad of IV in G; triad of V in G; diminished seventh chord of B; triad of IV in G; part of the chord of the dominant ninth—the full chord would be D, F♯, A, C, E; triad of I in G; triad of IV in G; triad of I; dominant seventh; triad of I in G, changed by introduction of F♯ into dominant seventh chord in C. It is pleasant, at times, to end an interlude thus, pausing upon the dominant chord, that the singers may be in readiness, and then bringing in the first chord of the tune as the resolution of the seventh chord.

The third interlude is adapted to the tune *Hebron* and should be analyzed by the learner.

(1) The learner is advised to study a little work entitled "A Guide to Composition" by H. Wohlfahrt.

The following interlude for the tune *Duke Street* may also be analyzed by the learner, with the exception of one chord, the fourth in the second measure, which has not been explained. *Duke Street* is written in different keys in the books in use. The interlude must, of course, be transposed, if played when the tune is in any other key than E♭.

The remaining interludes cannot be analyzed without further discussion of the laws of composition. They are contrapuntal,—that is, each of the parts has individuality,—in other words, is melodic.

For "DUKE STREET."

For "THE OLD HUNDREDTH."

The following interludes, adapted to the Old Hundredth, are constructed upon *motivos* from the tune. In the first one a *motivo* appears plainly in the Tenor part. In the second, a *motivo* is first heard in the Tenor, and then imitated in the other parts.

J. MOSENTHAL.

J. MOSENTHAL.

The learner should now form short passages of four, six, or eight measures each, using such chords only as have been explained, and adhering closely to the principles of succession laid down. Attempts to produce that which is new and original are futile, except for those who have made the art of composition a thorough study. Those who have learned only what is contained in this work, may do what thousands have done before them—that is, play short and simple passages within the scope of their present knowledge.

THEORETICAL DEPARTMENT.

CHAPTER I.

INTRODUCTION.

ANALYSIS OF TONES.

§ 96. *Distinctions observable in Tones.* Tones are readily distinguished as being relatively

1st, Long or Short.
2d, Low or High.
3d, Soft or Loud.[1]

§ 97. *Properties of Tones.* It follows from the above that every tone has three essential properties, or conditions of existence:

1st, Length.
2d, Pitch.
3d, Force.

§ 98. *Departments.* Hence it is convenient to divide rudiments of music into three departments: ·

1st, That which treats of Length . . . . RHYTHMICS.[2]
2d, That which treats of Pitch . . . . MELODICS.
3d, That which treats of Force . . . . DYNAMICS.

---

(1) Tones may be also distinguished as vocal or instrumental, good or bad, etc., but the three distinctions above named are all from which are derived the knowledge of the essential properties, or conditions of tones, or all that is requisite to their existence.

(2) *Rhythmics*, from a Greek word, signifying " to flow,"—measured movement. *Melodics*, from a Greek word, signifying " a song or poem,"—a tune. *Dynamics*, from a Greek word, signifying " to be able,"—power. The plural form of each of these words is taken as the name of a department, because as technical terms they comprehend everything that arises out of the properties of which they treat. Thus, Rhythmics comprehends *all rhythmic things*, or whatever may be derived from the primary fact that tones may be long or short, or that length is a property of tones, including also *rhythms*, or the structure of phrases, sections and periods. Again, the term Melodics includes everything that may proceed from the primary distinction of low or high, or from the property of pitch; the word melody, in its common use, is much more limited, and refers only to a pleasing succession of tones, or to a tune form. Dynamics also embraces not only the mere force of tones, but also their form of delivery.

CHAPTER II.

RHYTHMICS.

TONES. NOTES. RESTS.

§ 99. *Names of Tones.* Tones in this department are *named* by terms indicative of their relation in length or duration, as WHOLE, HALF, QUARTER, EIGHTH, SIXTEENTH, etc.

§ 100. *Representation of the relative length of Tones by Notes.* The relative length of tones is represented by characters called NOTES, the names of which correspond to those of the tones represented by them, as:

| *Whole,* | *Half,* | *Quarter,* | *Eighth,* | *Sixteenth,* etc.[3] |

§ 101. *Rests.* Characters corresponding to notes in re-·spect to length, and named from them, are used to indicate silence ; they are called RESTS.

§ 102. *Points of Addition.* A point of addition, or dot, adds one half to the length represented by a note or rest. Double dots add three quarters to the length represented by a note or rest.

§ 103. *Mark of Diminution.* A figure, employed as a mark of diminution, as 3, 5, 7, 9, &c., reduces the length represented by any three, five, seven, or nine equal notes to that of two, four, six, or eight of the same kind. Tones thus represented, and groups of notes thus marked, are called TRIPLETS, QUINTLETS, etc.

---

(3) The following names are often used instead of the above mentioned: Semibreve, Minim, Crotchet, Quaver, Semiquaver, Demisemiquaver, etc. Notes are also used in connection with the staff, to indicate the melodic or pitch succession of tones.

CHAPTER III.

RHYTHMICS.

MEASUREMENT OF TONES.

§ 104. *Measures.*—The relative length of tones is measured (compared or estimated) by a division of time into equal portions, called MEASURES, and PARTS OF MEASURES.[1]

§ 105. *Measures indicated.*—Measures and parts of measures may be conveniently indicated, *through the sense of hearing*, by counting ; and, *through the sense of seeing*, by certain motions of the hand called BEATS. Thus we are said to count or beat the time.

§ 106. *Different kinds of Measure and Accent.*—The following kinds of measure are in common use :—

1. A measure having two parts, accented on the first, is called DOUBLE MEASURE. It may be indicated by counting *one, two*.

2. A measure having three parts, accented on the first, is called TRIPLE MEASURE. It may be indicated by counting *one, two, three*.

3. A measure having four parts, accented principally on the first, and lightly on the third part, is called QUADRUPLE MEASURE. It may be indicated by counting *one, two, three, four*.

4. A measure having six parts, accented principally on the first, and lightly on the fourth part, is called SEXTUPLE MEASURE. It may be indicated by counting *one, two, three, four, five, six.*[2]

§ 107. *Syncope.*—When a tone commences on an *unaccented* part of a measure, and is continued on an *accented* part of a measure, the accent is inverted ; such a tone is called a SYNCOPE, or a SYNCOPATED TONE, and the note representing it is called a SYNCOPATED NOTE.[3]

§ 108. *Bars.*—Vertical lines are used in notation to mark the boundaries of written measures ; they are called BARS.

§ 109. *Double Bar.*—The end of a section or period, or the final close of a piece of music, or the end of a line in poetry, is often indicated by a DOUBLE BAR, or CLOSE.

§ 110. *Varieties of Measure.*—Parts of measures may be represented by any kind of notes, as half, quarter, eighth, etc., thus producing VARIETIES of MEASURE.[1]

§ 111. *Designation of the kind and variety of Measure.*—Both the *kind* and the *variety* of measure are designated by figures, as in the representation of fractions, the numerator referring to the *kind*, and the denominator to the *variety*.

CHAPTER IV.

MELODICS.

KEYS. SCALES. THE STAFF.

§ 112. *Keys, The Tonic.*—Tones that agree, and produce a pleasing effect, either in succession or combination, are related to each other, and form families or systems, which, collectively, are called KEYS. In every Key there is one tone more prominent than the others, which, in the shortest passages, and even when omitted may be felt to influence them, and is the only one upon which a long succession or series may satisfactorily end. It is called the TONIC or KEY-TONE.[2] The qualities of the tonic are not inherent in the tone itself, but depend upon its association with the component tones of its key. Every tone therefore becomes a tonic whenever the tones of its Key are employed.

§ 113. *Scales.*—When the tones of a Key are arranged in progressive order, ascending by regular gradations from the tonic, or descending to it they form what is called a DIATONIC SCALE.[3] There are two kinds of Diatonic scales, major and the minor, and twelve scales of each kind.

§ 114. *Number and Names of Scale-tones.*—Each scale consists of eight successive tones ascending, or descending. These are named from numbers. The Key-tone is called ONE. Those, above it, in ascending series are TWO, THREE, FOUR, FIVE, SIX, SEVEN, EIGHT.

---

(1) Measures and parts of measures are to music what days, months and years (also equal portions of time) are to the common occupations of life, or to history. They are the standard of measurement.

(2) Other kinds of measure are sometimes used, but further explanation is unnecessary.

(3) SYNCOPE, from two Greek words, signifying " to cut into," or " to cut off." A syncope cuts into, breaks up, contradicts, or violates the regular order of accent. While it is important that rhythmic accent should be observed, its constant mechanical, or drum-like recurrence is stiff, ungraceful, and repulsive to good taste. Such an accent belongs mostly to music of an inferior character, or to that which makes its appeal in the mere external sense, calling forth, perhaps, in a public assembly, and even sometimes in a concert-room, a disagreeable rhythmic drumming

or stamping with the feet. The march and the dance are much dependent upon it, though in the better forms of these classes of music, it is often concealed by higher properties for a short time, or as long as the feet may be trusted without it. Rhetorical accent or emphasis, or that which belongs to emotion, expression, or to poetical thoughts or ideas, on the contrary, is essential to a tasteful or appropriate performance, and should receive much attention. The common rules for accent are, therefore, liable to many exceptions.

(1) Varieties of measure merely furnish different signs for the same thing. To the ear they are the same, to the eye only do they differ ; the movement or degree of quickness depending not on the kind of notes, which represent no positive but only a relative length.

(2) This tone is very frequently called the KEY-NOTE, the word note being used in the sense of tone.

(3) Scale from the Latin *Scala*, signifying a ladder. Diatonic from two Greek words, *Dia* and *Tonus*, signifying through the tones, or from tone to tone.

§ 115. *The Staff.*—Scales are indicated by a character, consisting of five parallel, horizontal lines, together with their intermediate spaces, called THE STAFF.

§ 116. Each line and each space of the Staff is called A DEGREE (place or position by which the scale-pitch may be represented); thus the staff contains nine degrees, there being five lines and four spaces.

§ 117. When more degrees than nine are needed, lines and spaces above or below the Staff are used, called LINES ABOVE, or SPACES ABOVE, or LINES BELOW, or SPACES BELOW.

§ 118. Any degree of the staff may be fixed upon to indicate the tone One; but when this is determined the others must follow in proper order.

§ 119. The position of the scale is represented, and also the melodic succession of tones is indicated by notes written upon the staff.[1]

CHAPTER V.

MELODICS.

ABSOLUTE PITCH. MODEL SCALE. CLEFS.

§ 120. *Absolute Pitch.*—Pitch, considered independently of scale relationship, is called ABSOLUTE. It is named from letters, and is designated by them, as A, B, C, D, E, F, G.

§ 121. *The model Scale.*—That major scale, whose tones are produced by the white keys of the Piano-forte, and which is indicated in the notation more simply than the others, and therefore is usually learned first, is based upon C. C is One, D is Two, E is Three, F is Four, G is Five, A is Six, B is Seven, C is Eight.[2]

§ 122. Absolute pitch is connected with the staff *representatively* by the application of one of the letters, which, when thus used, is called a CLEF.[3]

§ 123. There are two clefs (clef-letters) in common use, F and G.[4]

(1) Notes are primarily rhythmic characters, indicating length; but they are also used for the above-named purpose. It should be understood, however, that it is only the length and order of succession of tones which are indicated by them; the pitch-relation being indicated exclusively by the staff. The note *itself* indicates length, and the degree of the staff, on which it is placed, indicates pitch.

(2) C is taken again for eight, because, when the scale is extended, the same tone which is eight in its relation to the tones below it, becomes one in relation to those which are above it.

(3) Clef (French) signifying key; thus, the clef is a key, clue, or guide to absolute pitch.

(4) Formerly all the seven letters were used, being written together at the commencement of the staff.

§ 124. *The F Clef.*—The F clef is placed upon the *fourth* line, and designates F as the pitch indicated by that line; consequently C (One of the model, or C scale) must, in this case, be indicated by the second space.[1]

§ 125. *The G Clef.*—The G clef is placed upon the *second* line, and designates G as the pitch indicated by that line; consequently C (One of the model, or C scale) must, in this case, be indicated by the line below.

CHAPTER VI.

MELODICS.

UPPER AND LOWER SCALES.

§ 126. The tone called EIGHT is also ONE of a scale above it, and eight of that scale is also one of a scale still higher. The tone called ONE is also Eight of a scale below it, and one of that scale is eight of a scale still lower. All these higher and lower scales belong to the same key, and with a slight modification of pitch, are severally duplicates one of another, their component tones being named relatively and absolutely alike.[2]

§ 127. *Entire Scale of Tones.*—The entire compass, or great scale of sounds appreciable by the human ear, consists of nine octaves, including one hundred and eight tones (more or less), which may be thus represented.[3]

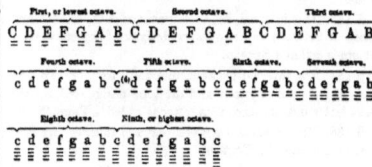

First, or lowest octave.   Second octave.   Third octave.

C D E F G A B C D E F G A B C D E F G A B

Fourth octave.   Fifth octave.   Sixth octave.   Seventh octave.

c d e f g a b c''''d e f g a b c d e f g a b c d e f g a b

Eighth octave.   Ninth, or highest octave.

c d e f g a b c d e f g a b c

(1) It should be understood that a clef is merely a letter differing in shape from its ordinary form.

(2) Tones are produced by vibrations; those of the Piano-forte by vibrations of strings. The ear is effected by the actual *rapidity of vibrations* (absolute pitch; than by *ratios of vibrations* (relative pitch.) Thus, the ear is comparatively indifferent as to whether the tones called One, Two and Three are produced by 24, 27, and 30, or, an octave higher, by 48, 54 and 60, or, an octave higher still, by 96, 108 and 120 vibrations in a given time; but it imperatively demands that the ratio between One and Two shall be as 24 to 27, and the ratio between Two and Three as 27 to 30.

(3) It is not intended to state with exactness the full compass or extent of tone-range; the number depends upon the perceptive power of the human ear. By some writers, the number is extended to one hundred and twenty, or more. In estimating the number of tones, the intermediate tones are, of course, included.

(4) This once marked small c, being about the center of the great range or compass, is called middle c.

§ 128. *Compass of the Piano-forte.*—The usual compass of the Piano-forte consists of about seven octaves, extending from A to a, or from C to c.

§ 129. *Absolute Pitch of the Clef Letters.*—The F clef indicates the small f in the fourth octave of the entire compass of tones, and the G clef indicates the small once-marked g in the fifth octave.

CHAPTER VII.

M E L O D I C S.

INTERVALS.

§ 130. *Intervals.*—The difference of Pitch between any two tones is called an INTERVAL.

§ 131. Intervals are reckoned by counting the degrees of the staff, or the letters which designate tones, always from the lower tone to the higher, unless otherwise expressed.

DIATONIC INTERVALS.[1]

§ 132. Between two tones of the same pitch there is no interval; such tones are called UNISON, or said to be in UNISON.

§ 133. The interval between one and two, or two and three, or between any two tones designated by contiguous letters is called a SECOND.

§ 134. The interval between one and three, or two and four, or between any tone and the tone designated by the next letter but one above its letter is called a THIRD.[2]

§ 135. The interval between one and four, or two and five, etc., is called a FOURTH.

§ 136. The interval between one and five, or two and six, etc., is called a FIFTH.

§ 137. The interval between one and six, or two and seven, etc., is called a SIXTH.

§ 138. The interval between one and seven, or two and eight, etc., is called a SEVENTH.

§ 139. The interval between one and eight, or two and nine (two of the next series), etc., is an OCTAVE.

(1) Diatonic, because produced by skips in diatonic scales.

(2) When the order of the tones of an interval is reversed, it is said to be inverted. Thus the interval *one* to *two*, a Second, becomes, when inverted, still reckoning from the lower tone to the higher, *two* to *one*, a Seventh. *One* to *three*, a Third becomes, when inverted, *three* to *one*, a Sixth. And so on.

CHAPTER VIII.

M E L O D I C S.

CHROMATIC SCALE.   CHROMATIC INTERVALS.

§ 140. *The Chromatic Scale.*—A series of tones, produced upon the Piano-forte by playing in succession all the black and white keys in an octave, is called THE CHROMATIC SCALE.[1] It has no key-tone. and may commence or end with any tone.

§ 141. *Tones produced by Black keys.*—The tones produced by the Black keys are named from those produced by the white keys between which the black ones occur, with the addition of either the word sharp or flat affixed. Thus the tone between C and D is named C SHARP or D FLAT. The same principle is applied to the naming of the tones of all the other black keys.

§ 142. The tones of the black keys are indicated by modifications of those degrees of the staff from which they are named; thus the tone named C sharp is indicated by the same degree of the staff as the tone named C, but modified by a character prefixed to it, called a SHARP ($\sharp$). So also the tone named A flat is indicated by the same degree of the staff as the tone named A, but modified by a character prefixed to it. called a FLAT ($\flat$). The same principle of modification is applied to certain tones that are produced by white keys; thus the tone named C is sometimes indicated by the same degree of the staff as the tone named B, but modified by a sharp prefixed to it. This principle of modification is also carried still further; thus the tone named G is sometimes indicated by the same degree of the staff as the tone named F, but modified by a character prefixed to it, called a DOUBLE SHARP (𝄪).

§ 143. *The effect of Sharps and Flats*, in Piano-forte music, may therefore be stated as follows:[2] When a sharp is

(1) *Chromatic.*—From a Greek word, signifying *color*. It is said that the intermediate tones were formerly represented by notes written with colored ink, and hence the name. The term may also have a figurative meaning, since chromatics in music, expressive of various degrees of intensity of feeling, may be regarded as analogous to the light and shade, or coloring in painting.

(2) The use of these characters furnishes *three* names to every key but one of the twelve in the octave, as exhibited in the following diagram:

B𝄪	F♭♭			E𝄪	A♭	C♭♭	
Db	Eb			F♯	G♯	Bb	
C♯	D♯			Gb		A𝄪	

Dbb	Ebb	Fb	Gbb	Abb	Bbb	Cb	Dbb
B♯	C𝄪	D𝄪	E♯	F𝄪	G𝄪	A𝄪	B♯
C	D	E	F	G	A	B	C

employed, the key to be struck is always the next one, black or white, to the right of that one which should be struck if there were no sharp. When a Flat is employed the next key, black or white, to the left, is to be struck. When a double sharp is used the next key but one to the right is to be struck. A double flat (♭♭) indicates the next key but one to the left.

§ 144. The significance of a flat or sharp, unless it is in the signature (See § 154), extends only through the measure in which it occurs.

§ 145. The significance of a flat or sharp is terminated by a character called a NATURAL,(♮)[1] which always indicates a white key.

MAJOR, MINOR, DIMINISHED, AND AUGMENTED INTERVALS.

§ 146. *Seconds.*—1. A second, consisting of tones produced by two contiguous keys of the Piano-forte, black or white, is called a MINOR (small) SECOND. 2. A second, consisting of tones produced by any key, and the next key but one *to the right* of it, black or white; or, in which one key, black or white, is skipped between that producing the lower tone and that producing the higher, is a MAJOR (large) SECOND. 3. A second, in which two keys, black or white, are skipped, is an AUGMENTED SECOND.

§ 147. *Thirds.*—1. A third, in which one key is skipped, is DIMINISHED. 2. A third, in which two keys, black or white, are skipped, is MINOR. 3. A third, in which three keys, black and white, are skipped, is MAJOR.

§ 148. *Fourths.*—1. A fourth, in which three keys are skipped, is DIMINISHED. 2. A fourth, in which four keys are skipped, is PERFECT. 3. A fourth, in which five keys are skipped, is AUGMENTED.

§ 149. *Fifths.*—1. A fifth, in which five keys are skipped, is DIMINISHED. 2. A fifth, in which six keys are skipped, is PERFECT. 3. A fifth, in which seven keys are skipped, is AUGMENTED.

§ 150. *Sixths.*—1. A sixth, in which seven keys are skipped, is MINOR. 2. A sixth, in which eight keys are skipped, is MAJOR. 3. A sixth, in which nine keys are skipped, is AUGMENTED.

§ 151. *Sevenths.*—1. A seventh, in which eight keys are skipped, is DIMINISHED. 2. A seventh, in which nine keys are skipped, is MINOR. 3. A seventh, in which ten keys are skipped, is MAJOR.

§ 152. *Octave.*—An octave, in which eleven keys are skipped, is PERFECT.

(1) The name of this character is an unfortunate one, since its tendency is to mislead the pupil. It signifies not that one tone is in fact more natural than another—indeed the term cannot be said to apply to the tone, but merely to the previous mark (flat or sharp), showing that its significance is now at an end. If it was called a CANCEL, its name would more clearly indicate its office.

CHAPTER IX.

MELODICS.

MAJOR SCALES THAT REQUIRE BLACK KEYS.

§ 153. *Order of Intervals in Major Scales.*—All the Major Scales conform to a certain *law* in the order of the intervals between their tones. Any tone of the chromatic scale may be taken as ONE; the other tones follow, in ascending, each a Major second above the preceding, except *four*, which is only a Minor second above three, and *eight*, which is only a Minor second above seven. The following formula exhibits this order to the eye :

$$\text{I, } \overset{\text{s}}{\underset{\text{s}}{\text{II, }}} \overset{\text{s}}{\underset{\text{s}}{\text{III, IV, }}} \overset{\text{s}}{\underset{\text{s}}{\text{V, }}} \overset{\text{s}}{\underset{\text{s}}{\text{VI, }}} \overset{\text{s}}{\underset{\text{s}}{\text{VII, VIII.}}}^{(1)}$$

The white keys of the Piano-forte produce the tones of the key of C[2] in exact conformity to this law, but all the other scales require one or more black keys; the notation also is so arranged that the scale of C is indicated without sharps or flats, while all other keys require one or more of them.

§ 154. *The Signature.*—Each key is noted at the commencement of the staff, immediately after the clef, by sharps or flats, indicative of its component tones. Such an indication of the key is called THE SIGNATURE.

§ 155. The relative order of succession of keys, together with the signature of each, is exhibited in the following table :[3]

FIRST.—Each key a fifth above the preceding key.

Key of G. Signature, one sharp, or F♯.

Key of D. Signature, two sharps, or F♯ and C♯.

Key of A. Signature, three sharps, or F♯, C♯ and G♯.

Key of E. Signature, four sharps, or F♯, C♯, G♯ and D♯.

Key of B. Signature, five sharps, or F♯, C♯, G♯, D♯ and A♯.

Key of F♯. Signature, six sharps, or F♯, C♯, G♯, D♯, A♯ and E♯.

Key of C♯. Signature, seven sharps, or F♯, C♯, G♯, D♯, A♯, E♯ and B♯.

(1) Roman numerals are used throughout this work to indicate SCALE-RELATIONSHIP.

(2) The key of C has usually been called *natural*, or the *natural key*, but since the term natural, as here used, refers not to the scale itself, but to the mere notation of the scale; and since the key of C is, in reality, no more natural than any other; we prefer to follow the example of those modern writers on music who have, with much propriety, designated it as the MODEL key.

(3) Those keys, which have the greatest number of tones in common, are said to be the nearest related ; for example, the key of C has all its tones in common with the key of G but one, viz., F ; and the key of G has all its tones in common with the key of C but one, viz. F♯; hence, these two keys are nearly related ; so also of other keys.

SECOND.— Each key a fourth above the preceding key.

Key of F. Signature, one flat, or B♭.

Key of B♭. Signature, two flats, or B♭ and E♭.·

Key of E♭. Signature, three flats, or B♭, E♭ and A♭.

Key of A♭. Signature, four flats, or B♭, E♭, A♭ and D♭.

Key of D♭. Signature, five flats, or B♭, E♭, A♭, D♭ and G♭.

Key of G♭. Signature, six flats, or B♭, E♭, A♭, D♭, G♭ and C♭.

Key of C♭.[1] Signature, seven flats, or B♭, E♭, A♭, D♭, G♭, C♭ and F♭.

CHAPTER X.

M E L O D I C S.

MINOR SCALES.

§ 156. *Order of Intervals in Minor Scales.*—Minor Scales differ from Major Scales in the order of the intervals between their tones. There are different forms in common use.

First Form: (*The Harmonic Minor Scale.*)

I, Key omitted. II, III, Key omitted. IV, Key omitted. V, VI, Two keys omitted. VII, VIII.

The model scale in this form consists of the tones— A, B, C, D, E, F, G♯, A.

Second Form. (*The Melodic Minor Scale.*)

I, Key omitted. II, III, Key omitted. IV, Key omitted. V, Key omitted. VI, Key omitted. VII, VIII.

This form is Minor only in its lower tones, the upper part of the scale being Major. It is commonly used only in ascending, the scale taking-the first form in descending. The model scale in this form consists of the tones—A, B, C, D, E, F♯, G♯, A.

§ 157. It is not customary to write signatures for the Minor scales fully indicative of their component tones. Each Minor scale is so nearly identical with some one major scale that the signature of the Major key, with an accidental sharp or natural for seven, and in some forms also for six, is sufficient to indicate the Minor key.

§ 158. *Parallel Minor and Major.*—Minor and major scales which are indicated by the same signature, are said to be PARALLEL (or relative) each to the other.

---

(1) D♭ indicates the same key as C♯; F♯ the same as G♭, and B the same as C♭. Both ways of noting these keys are employed by composers.

§ 159. SIX (VI) of each Major scale is ONE (I) of its parallel Minor; THREE (III) of each Minor scale is ONE (I) of its parallel Major.

§ 160. The relative order of succession of keys together with the signature of each, is exhibited in the following table.

FIRST.—Each key a fifth above the preceding key.

Key of E Minor. Signature, one sharp, or F♯.

Key of B Minor. Signature, two sharps, or F♯ and C♯.

Key of F♯ Minor. Signature, three sharps, or F♯, C♯, and G♯.

Key of C♯ Minor. Signature, four sharps, or F♯, C♯, G♯, and D♯.

Key of G♯ Minor. Signature, five sharps, or F♯, C♯, G♯, D♯, and A♯.

Key of D♯ Minor. Signature, six sharps, or F♯, C♯, G♯, D♯, A♯, and E♯.

Key of A♯ Minor. Signature, seven sharps, or F♯, C♯, G♯, D♯ A♯ E♯ and B♯.

SECOND.—Each key a fourth above the preceding key.

Key of D Minor. Signature, one flat, or B♭.

Key of G Minor. Signature, two flats, or B♭, and E♭.

Key of C Minor. Signature, three flats, or B♭, E♭, and A♭.

Key of F Minor. Signature, four flats, or B♭, E♭, A♭, and D♭.

Key of B♭ Minor. Signature, five flats, or B♭, E♭, A♭, D♭, and G♭.

Key of E♭ Minor. Signature, six flats, or B♭, E♭, A♭, D♭, G♭, and C♭.

Key of A♭ Minor. Signature, seven flats, or B♭, E♭, A♭, D♭, G♭, C♭, and F♭.

CHAPTER XI.

M E L O D I C S.

PASSING TONES. SHAKE AND TURN.

§ 161. Connecting tones, tasteful or graceful, are often introduced into a melody; they are called PASSING TONES. They are sometimes represented by notes of a smaller size than those in which the music is mostly written, though this distinction is not always observed.

§ 162. A passing tone, or group of passing tones, which is closely connected with the following essential accented tone, is called an APPOGGIATURA

§ 163. A passing tone, or group of passing tones, which is closely connected with the preceding essential accented tone is called an AFTER-TONE.

§ 164. A rapid alternation of a tone with the conjoint tone above it, at an interval of either a step or a half-step, is called a TRILL or SHAKE. It is indicated by the abbreviation *tr*.

§ 165. A tone struck in rapid succession, with the conjoint tones above and below it, so as to produce a winding or turning melodic motion or movement, is called a TURN. It has a variety of forms, and, when not written in full, is indicated by a sign, thus ∾.

CHAPTER XII.

DYNAMICS.

FORCE OF TONES.

§ 166. *Mezzo.*—A tone of medium force is called MEZZO (pronounced mét-so); such a tone is indicated by the term *mezzo, mez.*, or *m*.

§ 167. *Piano.*—A tone somewhat softer than Mezzo, or a soft tone, is called PIANO (pee-äh-no, or p'yáh-no), and is indicated by the term *piano, pia.*, or *p*.

§ 168. *Forte.*—A tone somewhat louder than Mezzo, or a loud tone, is called FORTE (fōre-tay, or fōre-te), and is indicated by the term *forte, for.* or *f*.

§ 169. *Pianissimo.*—A tone softer than Piano is called PIANISSIMO (pee-ah-nís-si-mo, or p'yah-nís-si-mo), and is indicated by *pp*.

§ 170. *Fortissimo.*—A tone louder than Forte is called FORTISSIMO (fōrtis'-si-mo), and is indicated by *ff*.[1]

CHAPTER XIII.

DYNAMICS.

FORMS OF TONES.

§ 171. Although tones cannot be long-sustained upon the Piano-forte, yet, by rapid reiteration and otherwise, effects analogous to those produced by the different forms of vocal tones are often heard from the instrument.

§ 172. *Organ Form.*[2]—A tone or passage commenced, continued, and ended with an equal degree of force, is called an ORGAN FORM, or an ORGAN TONE. It may be indicated by parallel lines, thus: ═══

§ 173. *Crescendo.*—A tone or passage commencing Piano, and gradually increasing to Forte, is called CRESCENDO (cre-shén-do). It is indicated by *cres.*, or by two divergent lines, thus: ◁══

§ 174. *Diminuendo.*—A tone or passage commencing Forte, and gradually diminishing to Piano, is called DECRESCENDO or DIMINUENDO (de-cre-shén-do or dim-in-oo-én-do). It is indicated by *decres., dim.*, or by two convergent lines, thus: ══▷

§ 175. *Swell.*—A union of the Crescendo and Decrescendo produces the SWELL FORM: indicated by the union of the divergent and convergent lines, thus: ◁═▷

§ 176. *Sforzando.*—A tone which is produced very suddenly and forcibly, and instantly diminished, is called SFORZANDO, or FORZANDO (sfōrt-shán-do or fōrt-shéndo). It is designated thus >, or by *sf.*, or *fz*.

CHAPTER XIV.

HARMONY.

CONSTRUCTION OF CHORDS.

§ 177. *Chords.*—A combination of harmonious tones, simultaneously performed, is called a CHORD. Chords are reckoned, like intervals, by counting either the letters, which designate tones, or the degrees of the staff upward, from a certain tone, which is called the ROOT of the chord. Each chord is named from its root, and every conceivable arrangement of its component tones, receives the same name.

§ 178. *Triads.*—1. A chord composed of Root, Major Third, and Perfect Fifth, is called a MAJOR TRIAD. 2. A chord composed of Root, Minor Third, and Perfect Fifth, is called a MINOR TRIAD. 3. A chord composed of Root, Minor Third, and Diminished Fifth, is a DIMINISHED TRIAD.

There are *seven* different combinations of the musical letters, which, modified by sharps and flats, are sufficient to designate all possible triads. The following table exhibits them, with the first combination repeated several times to show its modifications. Some of them are seldom used.— The other triads may be modified in a similar manner.

(1) There are also modifications of the above mentioned degrees of force, as *Mezzo-Forte, Mezzo-Piano.* Mezzo, Piano, and Forte are Italian words which are universally used as technical terms in music. The instrument called the Piano-Forte derives its name from these words. It should not be called Piano-*Fōrt*, but Piano-*Fōr*tay or Piano *Fōr*-te.

(2) The Organ Tone takes its name from the organ pipe, which can only produce a tone of one equal degree of power.

TABLE.

	Major.		Minor.			Dim.					
Fifths,	E	E♭	E	E♭	E♮	E♭	E	F	G	A	B	C	D
Thirds,	C♯	C	C	C♯	C♯	C	C♯	D	E	F	G	A	B
Roots,	A	A♭	A	A♭	A♯	A	A♯	B	C	D	E	F	G

§ 179. *Chords of the Seventh.*—1. A chord composed of Root, Major Third, Perfect Fifth and Minor Seventh, is called a CHORD OF THE DOMINANT SEVENTH. There are twelve such chords, one only for every key, whether Major or Minor. The Root is always V, (Five of the scale,) the third VII, the Fifth II, and the Seventh IV. 2. A chord composed of Root, Minor Third, Diminished Fifth, and Diminished Seventh, is called a CHORD OF THE DIMINISHED SEVENTH. There are, in name and to the eye, twelve such chords, one for every Minor key; but upon the key-board of the Piano-forte, and to the ear, there are only three of them. Each one belongs to four Minor keys. Thus, in A Minor, this chord is G♯ (VII), B (II), D (IV), F (VII). The same keys of the instrument produce the chord, which, in C Minor, is named B♮ (VII), D (II), F (IV), A♭ (VI); and, in F♯ Minor, is named E♯ (VII), G♯ (II), B (IV), D (VI); and again, in E♭ Minor, is named D♮ (VII), F (II), A♭ (IV), C♭ (VI).

§ 180.—The difference between Minor and Major keys is as clearly illustrated by chords, as by scales. Thus, the triad of I in the key of A Minor, is a Minor triad, A, C, E. The triad of I, in A Major, is a Major triad, A, C♯, E. The triad of IV, in A minor, is D, F, A ; in A Major, it is D, F♯, A. The triad of VI. in A Minor, is a Major triad F, A, C. The triad of VI, in A Major, is a Minor triad, F♯, A, C♯. The chord of the Dominant Seventh *is always the same in both Major and Minor keys.* In A, Major and Minor, it is E (V), G♯ (VII), B (II), and D (IV).

CHAPTER XV.

HARMONY.

SUCCESSIONS AND RESOLUTIONS OF CHORDS. (1.)

§ 181. *Successions of Triads.*—1. The Triad of V, may follow the Triad of I, or be followed by it, with a uniformly good effect. A great variety of simple Dance and Military music, is composed almost wholly of these two chords. (See Example No. 1, below.) 2. The Triad of IV may follow that of I, or be followed by it. 3. The Triad of IV may be followed by that of V, provided the interval of a perfect fifth is not so placed in the latter chord as to produce an unpleasant effect. 4. The Triad of VI may follow that of I, and be followed by that of IV, with good effect. All these successions may be used in every Major and Minor key.

(1) To discuss fully the principles involved in SUCCESSIONS OF CHORDS would require a volume, and is entirely beyond the scope of this work. A few only of the most simple progressions and resolutions, which can easily be produced upon the key-board by pupils, are deemed sufficient.

(2) The word *part* is here used technically, to designate a single succession of tones which might, for example, be sung by a voice simultaneously with one or more other successions, either sung or played.

EXAMPLES.

KEY OF C MAJOR.

KEY OF C MINOR.

§ 182. *The principles involved* in the successions of chords shown in the foregoing examples, are as follows:

1. When a note belongs to two successive chords it is written in the same part in the second chord as in the first. For example : G belongs to both the first and second chords of No. 1. It is placed in the Alto in the second chord because it is there in the first; thus it connects the two chords together. 2. When a chord contains no note that belongs to the preceding chord, contrary motion of the parts—the Base ascending and the upper parts descending, or the reverse,—is employed. For example : the second chord in No. 3 is F, A, C, and the third chord is G, B, D. There is no note that belongs to both chords. Contrary motion is much more pleasing than would be parallel motion, thus :

§ 183. *Resolution.*—Chords of the seventh, unlike triads, do not produce satisfactory effects by themselves, but demand to be followed by other chords upon which they are said to *Resolve*.

§ 184. *Resolution of the Dominant Seventh chord.*—The Dominant Seventh chord may be resolved upon the triad of I, or the triad of VI, Major or Minor.

LAW OF RESOLUTION UPON THE TRIAD OF I.

1. The *Root* of the dominant, when in the Base, ascends or descends to the root of the triad; when in either of the other parts it remains and becomes the fifth of the triad. 2. The *Third* ascends to the root of the triad. 3. The *Fifth*, generally descends to the root of the triad. 4. The *Seventh* descends to the third of the triad. In the key of C Major or Minor, for example,

The Seventh, F, is followed by E or E♭.
The Fifth, D, is followed by C.
The Third, B, is followed by C.
The Root, G, is followed, in an upper part, by G.
The Root, G, is followed, in the Base, by C.

KEY OF C MAJOR.

Root in the Base.   *Third of the Dom. Chord in the Base.*

Fifth of Dom. Chord in Base.   *Seventh of Dom. Chord in Base.*

KEY OF C MINOR.

LAW OF RESOLUTION UPON THE TRIAD OF VI.

1. The *Root*, and *Third* of the dominant, ascend to the root and third of the triad. 2. The *Fifth* and *Seventh* descend to the third and fifth of the triad. In the key of C, Major and Minor, for example,

The Seventh, F, is followed by E or E♭.
The Fifth, D, is followed by C.
The Third, B, is followed by C.
The Root, G, is followed by A or A♭.

KEY OF C MAJOR.   KEY OF C MINOR.

§ 185. *Resolution of the Diminished Seventh Chord.*—The Diminished Seventh chord may be resolved upon the triad of I in the Minor key. Its law of resolution is the same as that of the dominant seventh upon the triad of VI.

KEY OF C MINOR.

CHAPTER XVI.

THEORY OF FINGERING.

INTRODUCTION.—ANALYSIS OF PASSAGES.

§ 186. *Classes of Passages.*—Although compositions for the Piano-forte are innumerable, yet analysis shows that in regard to fingering, the materials composing them may all be arranged into THREE PRINCIPAL CLASSES, and that certain general rules for playing may be given, which, though subject to exceptions, are mainly correct, and greatly assist the learner. ·

1. The First Class comprises all passages in which, while the body of the hand is held quiet in one position, the fingers play the keys directly under them. 2. The Second Class comprises Scales, and all passages derived or formed from scales. 3. The Third Class comprises Chords, and all passages derived or formed from chords.

CHAPTER XVII.

CLASSES OF PASSAGES. GENERAL RULES.

§ 187. *First Class.*—This class includes the FIVE FINGER passages—so called because the hand covers five keys, and each finger plays only the key directly under it; also those in which the fingers extend over six, seven, or eight keys, and play the keys under them while the body of the hand remains unmoved. It includes likewise those passages in which the position of the hand is frequently changed by CONTRACTION or EXTENSION, and the INTERLOCKING passages, in which one hand constantly passes over the other to a new position.

§ 188. THE FIRST GENERAL RULE requires that the hand should never move without a reason, and that, when it does change its position, it should instantly fit itself to the keys to be played.

§ 189. *The Second Class* includes all the Scales and scale passages, as follows :

1. *The Chromatic Scale.*—In this scale the black keys are played by the second finger, and the white keys by the thumb except in those places where two white keys have no black one between them ; there C and F are played by the first finger of the right hand, and E and B by the first finger of the left.

2. *Major and Minor Diatonic Scales.*—The Diatonic Scales, when played singly—one key by each hand—are all fingered upon the same principles: thumb, first, and second, or second, first, and thumb, are always used twice, and the third finger once, in every octave ; it follows that, in every

scale, if the third finger takes its proper key the other fingers will easily fall into their places. The following tables, showing the keys struck by the *third fingers* indicate sufficiently the whole fingering of these scales.

MAJOR SCALES.

Third of Right on.	B	F♯	C♯	G♯	D♯	A♯	A♯	A♯	B♭	B♭	B♭	B♭
Scale of	C	G	D	A	E	B	F♯	C♯	A♭	E♭	B♭	F
Third of Left on...	D	A	E	B	F♯	F♯	F♯	F♯	D♭	A♭	E♭	G

(1)

MINOR SCALES.

Third of Right on.	B♮	F♯	C♯	G♯	D♯	A♯	D	A	B♭	B♭	B♭
Scale of	C	G	D	A	E	B	F♯	C♯	F	B♭	E♭	A♭
Third of Left on...	D	A	E	B	F♯	F♯	F♯	F♯	G	C♭	G♭	G

§ 3. *Diatonic Scales in Double Thirds.*—In playing the scales in Double Thirds—two keys by each hand at the interval of a third—alternate fingers move in pairs, thumb with second, first with third, and second with fourth. No other combination is used. Once only, in each octave, the second and *fourth* are employed ; it follows that if the *fourth* finger takes its proper key in every scale the other fingers will easily fall into their places. The following tables indicate the fourth-finger keys.

MAJOR SCALES.

Fourth of Right on.	G	D	A	E	B	F♯	F♯	F♯	G	G	G	G
Scale of	C	G	D	A	E	B	F♯	C♯	F	B♭	E♭	A♭
Fourth of Left on.	C	D	A	A	A	A♯	A♯	A♯	F	G	C	F

MINOR SCALES.

Fourth of Right on.	C	D	E	B	B	A♯	E♯	B♯	G	G♭	G♭	G
Scale of	C	G	D	A	E	B	F♯	C♯	F	B♭	E♭	A♭
Fourth of Left on.	C	G	G	E	A	A♯	A	A	F	B♭	C♭	F♮

4. *The Chromatic Scale in Double Thirds,* having more tones than the Diatonic, requires the fourth finger to be used twice in each octave ; in Minor thirds on E, and A, with the Right hand, and on C and G, with the Left ; in Major thirds on F, and B♭, with the Right hand, and on G♭, and B♮, with the Left. (See Figure 41, (a) and (b).)

5. *Diatonic Scales in Double Sixths.* — In playing the scales in double sixths—two keys by each hand at the interval of a sixth—the *thumb* and *third* finger, and the *first* and

(1) Another mode of fingering, which has the great advantage of perfect uniformity, and is therefore easily remembered, places the third finger of the Left hand on G or G♭ in all the scales that are written with flats. Another mode still, places the third finger of the Left hand upon VII, in the scales of D♭, E♭, and A♭. Neither of these, however, is quite so well adapted to playing with the greatest rapidity as the old fingering.

fourth fingers alternate. Once only in the octave the *thumb* and *second* are used. The key played by the *second finger* is, therefore, the guide to the entire fingering of each scale. The following tables indicate the second-finger keys.

MAJOR SCALES.

Second of Right on.	E	E	B	F♯	C♯	G♯	G♯	A	A	A♭	A♭
Scale of............	C	G	D	A	E	B	F♯	C♯	F	B♭	E♭	A♭
Second of Left on..	G	G	G	G♯	G♯	G♯	G♯	G♯	C	F	B♭	E♭

MINOR SCALES.

Second of Right on	D	E♭	B♭	F	E	B	F♯	C♯	E♮	A♮	A♭	A♭
Scale of...........	C	G	D	A	E	B	F♯	C♯	F	B♭	E♭	A♭
Second of Left on..	B♮	F♯	C♯	A	E	G	G♯	G♯	E♮	A♮	F	E♭

6. *The Chromatic Scale in Double Sixths* requires the second finger to be used twice in each octave, on C, or C♯ and G, or G♯, with the Right hand, and E, or E♭, and A,° or A♭, with the Left.

Figure 41 gives a condensed view of the Chromatic scale in Major and Minor Thirds, and Major and Minor Sixths with the fingering already described. It also exhibits another fingering for the Thirds which was employed by CHOPIN, and is very useful in certain passages.

Figure 41.

(a) MINOR THIRDS.

(b) MAJOR THIRDS.

MINOR THIRDS.

MAJOR THIRDS.

MAJOR SIXTHS.

MINOR SIXTHS.

§ 190. THE SECOND GENERAL RULE requires that all passages of the second class should be fingered like the scales from which they are derived : Major passages like Major scales, Minor passages like Minor scales, and Chromatic passages, however short, like the Chromatic scale.

§ 191. *The third Class of Passages* includes all chords and their derivatives.

1. *Triads*, in their simplest form, are fingered by thumb, first and third or fourth, or thumb, second and fourth, with exceptions for places where first, second and fourth are more convenient. A well-trained hand will easily manage them without being guided by deffinite rules. Triads with one tone doubled—taken twice at the interval of an octave—are fingered by thumb, first, *second* and fourth, or thumb, first, *third* and fourth. The choice between the second and third depends upon the position of the key between the first and fourth fingers. If it is nearer the fourth than the first, or equi-distant, the third is taken ; if nearer the first, the second is used.

2. *Broken Triads. Tremolos.* When the component tones of a Triad are struck, successively or alternately, forming groups of tones within one octave, they are fingered as though they were struck together.

3. *Chords of the Seventh*, when struck simultaneously, successively or alternately in groups, within the limit of an octave, are fingered upon the same general principles as Triads.

4. *Arpeggios.*—When the component tones of a chord are struck successively through more than one octave, the series resulting is called an ARPEGGIO. Arpeggios are fingered like the chords from which they are derived, except, that once in the octave, the thumb is used, instead of the fourth finger, to secure the new position of the hand.

§ 192. THE THIRD GENERAL RULE requires that all groups and passages of the third class, should be fingered as nearly as possible like the chords from which they are derived.

DICTIONARY OF MUSICAL TERMS.

A, (*Italian.*) By, for.

A CAPRICCIO, (*It.*) In accordance with the fancy of the performer.

ACCENT, Stress or force upon a tone. It is sometimes indicated by a sign (⸌).

ACCELERANDO, (*It.*) With constantly increasing speed.

ACCENTUATO, (*It.*) Strongly accented.

ACCOMPANIMENT. A part added to a principal one by way of enhancing the effect of the composition.

ADAGIO, (*It.*) A very slow degree of movement.

ADAGISSIMO, (*It.*) Extremely slow.

AD LIBITUM, (*Latin.*) At will, or discretion. This expression implies that the time of some particular passage is left to the pleasure of the performer, or, that he is at liberty to introduce whatever embellishments his fancy may suggest.

AFFETTUOSO, (*It.*) Affectionate, tender.

AGITATO, CON AGITAZIONE, (*It.*) With agitation, anxiously.

AL, ALL', ALLA, (*It.*) To the; *sometimes,* in the style of.

ALLEGREMENTE, (*It.*) With quickness.

ALLEGRETTO, (*It.*) Somewhat cheerful, but not so quick as *allegro.*

ALLEGRETTO SCHERZANDO, (*It.*) Moderately playful and vivacious.

ALLEGREZZA, (*It.*) Joy; as, *con allegrezza,* joyfully.

ALLEGRISSIMO, (*It.*) Extremely quick and lively.

ALLEGRO, (*It.*) Quick, lively. A term implying a rapid and vivacious movement, but which is frequently modified by the addition of other words; as, *allegro agitato,* quick, with anxiety and agitation; *allegro con brio,* brilliantly quick; *allegro furioso,* furiously quick, &c.

AL SEGNO, (*It.*) AL SEG., or the character 𝄋, signifies that the performer must return to a similar character in the course of the movement, and play from that place to the word *fine,* or to the mark ⌒ over a double bar.

ANDANTE, (*It.*) Implies a movement somewhat slow and sedate. This term is often modified, both as to time and style, by the addition of other words.

ANDANTINO, (*It.*) Somewhat quicker than *andante.*

ANIMATO, CON ANIMA, ANIMOSO, (*It.*) With animation, in a spirited manner.

A PIACERE, A PIACIMENTO, (*It.*) At the pleasure of the performer.

APPOGGIATURA, (*It.*) A note of embellishment, generally written in a small character.

A QUATRE MAINS, (*French.*) For four hands.

APPOGGIATO, (*It.*) Dwelt, leaned upon.

ARIA, (*It.*) An air or song.

ARIOSO, (*It.*) In the style of an air.

ARPEGGIANDO, ⎱ (*It.*) Passages formed of the
ARPEGGIATO, ⎰ tones of chords taken in rapid
ARPEGGIO, ⎰ succession, in imitation of the harp, are said to be in *arpeggio.*

ASSAI, (*It.*) Very, extremely. This adverb is always joined to some other word, of which it extends the signification; as, *adagio assai,* very slow; *allegro assai,* very quick.

A TEMPO, ⎱ (*It.*) In the regular time.
A TEM, ⎰

A TEMPO GIUSTO, (*It.*) In strict and equal time.

ATTACCA, ATTACCA SUBITO, (*It.*) Implies that the performer must directly commence the following movement.

BALLAD, A short and familiar song.

BARCAROLLE, (*It.*) Airs sung by the Venetian gondoliers or boatmen.

BEN, (*It.*) Well; as, BEN MARCATO, (*It.*) Well marked. This expression indicates that the passage must be executed in a clear, distinct, and strongly accented manner.

BIS, (*Lat.*) Twice. A term which indicates that a certain passage, distinguished by a curve drawn over or under it, must be performed twice.

BRAVURA, (*It.*) An air calculated to display execution, and requiring a bold and splendid performance.

BRILLANTE, (*It. and Fr.*) An expression indicating a showy and sparkling style of performance.

BRIO, CON BRIO, ⎱ (*It.*) With brilliancy and spirit.
BRIOSO, ⎰

BRISE, (*Fr.*) Sprinkled, broken into arpeggios.

BUFFO, (*It.*) Comic.

BURLESCO, (*It.*) With ludicrous, burlesque humor.

CELERITA, (*It.*) Velocity.

CADENCE. A close in melody or harmony.

CADENZA, (*It.*) A graceful, ornamental passage, either extemporaneous or written, generally introduced near the close of a regular composition.

CALANDO, (*It.*) Gradually diminishing in tone and quickness.

CALORE, (*It.*) With much warmth and animation.

CANONE, (*It.*) ⎱ A contrapuntal composition, in
CANON, ⎰ which one part follows another in exact uninterrupted imitation.

CANTABILE, (*It.*) In a graceful and singing style.

CANTANTE, (*It.*) A part to be executed by the voice.

CANTATA, (*It.*) A vocal composition, of several movements.

CANTO, (*It.*) The highest vocal part in choral music.

CAPELLA, ALLA, (*It.*) In the church style.

CAPO, (*It.*) The head, or beginning.

CAPRICCIO, (*It.*) A fanciful and irregular species of composition.

CAVATINA, (*It.*) An air of one movement or part only, occasionally preceded by a recitative.

CHANT, (*Fr.*) A song or melody; the vocal part.

CHE, (*It.*) Than; as, *poco più che andante,* rather slower than *andante.*

CHORAL. That which relates to a choir or chorus. A tune of a simple and uniform character, adapted to worship.

CHORD. A combination of harmonious tones simultaneously performed.

CHROMATIC. Proceeding by the smallest intervals practicable in Piano-forte music; in other words, from key to key, black or white.

CODA, (*It.*) A few measures added beyond the natural close of a composition, which may usually be omitted at pleasure.

COL, COLL', COLLA, (*It.*) These are different forms of the combination of *con,* (with) and *lo,* (the), meaning *with the,* as, *coll' arco* with the bow ; *col basso,* with the base, *colla parte,* with the part, *i. e.* the accompanist should play in time with principle part or voice.

COMMODO. Quietly, conveniently, as to movement.

CON, (*It.*) With; as, *con espressione,* with expression : *con brio,* with brilliancy and spirit.

CONCENTO, (*It.*) Concord, agreement. A selection of pieces is sometimes so called.

CONCERTO, (*It.*) A composition intended to display the powers of some particular instrument with orchestral accompaniments.

CON DOLCEZZA, (*It.*) With sweetness.

CON DOLORE, (*It.*) Mournfully, with pathos.

CON GRAVITA, (*It.*) With gravity.

CON GRAZIA, (*It.*) With grace.

CON GUSTO, GUSTOSO, (*It.*) With taste.

CON IMPETO, (*It.*) With impetuosity.

CON MOTO, (*It.*) In an agitated style, with spirit.

CON SPIRITO. (*It.*) With quickness and spirit.

COUNTERPOINT. The art of composing music in harmonious parts which have individuality.

CRESCENDO, or CRES., (*It.*) With a gradually increasing quantity of tone.

DA, (*It.*) By.

DA CAPO, or D. C., (*It.*) From the beginning; an expression which is often written at the end of a movement, to indicate that the performer must return to and finish with the first strain.

DAL, (*It.*) By ; as, *dal segno,* from the sign ; a mark of repetition.

DECRESCENDO, (*It.*) Gradually decreasing in quantity of tone.

DELICATO, (*It.*) ⎱ These terms imply a
DELICATAMENTE, (*It.*) ⎰ delicate and tasteful
DELICATEZZA, (*It.*) ⎰ performance.

DIATONIC, (*Greek.*) Naturally ; that is, according to the degrees of the major or minor scale.

DILUENDO, (*It.*) A gradual dying away of the tone till it arrives at extinction.

DIMINUENDO, (*It.*) Implies that the quantity of tone must be gradually diminished.

DI MOLTO, (*It.*) An expression which serves to augment the signification of the word to which it is added ; as, *allegro di molto,* very quick.

DIVERTIMENTO, (*It.*) A short, light composition, written in a familiar and pleasing style.

DOLCE, or DOL., (*It.*) Implies a soft and sweet style.

DOLCEZZA, or CON DOLCEZZA, (*It.*) With sweetness and softness.

DOLCEMENTE, (*It.*) In a sweet and graceful style.

DOLOROSO, (*It.*) Indicates a soft and pathetic style.

DOMINANT. The fifth tone of any scale.

DOPPIO, (*It.*) Double.

DOUX, (*Fr.*) Sweet, soft.

DYNAMICS. That department of musical theory which treats of the power or force of tones.

E, ED, The Italian conjunction *and;* as, *flauto e violino,* flute and violin ; *nobilmente ed animato,* with grandeur and spirit.

ELEGAMENTE, ⎱
ELEGANTE, ⎰ (*It.*) With elegance, gracefully.
ELEGANZA, ⎰

ENERGICO, CON ENERGIA, ENERGICAMENTE, (*It.*) With energy.

ENCORE, (*French.*) Again.

EQUALMENTE, (*It.*) Equally, evenly.

ESPRESSIVO, or CON ESPRESSIONE, (*It.*) With expression.

ESTRAVAGANZA, (*It.*) Extravagant and wild as to composition and performance.

ETUDE, (*French.*) A study. See §48, p. 58.

ET, (*Latin.*) And.

EXECUTION. This word is used technically to denote the ability to perform difficult passages with ease and rapidity.

EXTEMPORE, (*Latin.*) Without previous composing; unpremeditated.

FACILITA, (*It.*) A facilitation, an easier adaptation.

FANTAISIE, (*Fr.*) ⎱ A species of composition in
FANTASIA, (*It.*) ⎰ which the author gives free scope to his ideas, without regard to those systematic forms which regulate other compositions.

FINALE, The last piece of any act of an opera or of a concert; or the last movement of a symphony or sonata, in the German style.

FINE, (*It.*) The end.

FORTE, or FOR., or simply *f,* (*It.*) Loud.

FORTISSIMO, or *ff,* (*It.*) Very loud.

FORZANDO, or FORZ., or *fz,* implies that the note is to be marked with particular emphasis or force.

FORZA, (It.) Force; as, con forza, with force.

FUGUE. A contrapuntal composition, in which a subject, proposed by one part, is imitated by the others in accordance with certain laws.

FUOCO, CON, (It.) With intense animation.

FURIOSO, or CON FURIA, (It.) With fire.

GAIEMENT, (Fr.) In a cheerful and lively style.

GALLOPADE, (Fr.) }
GALOP, (Ger.) } A galop; a quick species of
GALLOPPE, (Fr.) } dance, generally in 2-4 time.

GIUSTO (It.) In just and exact time.

GLISSANDO, (It.) Gliding. This term is employed in certain Piano pieces to indicate a rapid sliding over white keys.—A mere trick to conceal the want of execution, and unworthy of an artist.

GRACES. Occasional embellishments, sometimes indicated by the composer, sometimes spontaneously introduced by the performer. The most important of these are the appoggiatura, the turn, and the trill.

GRANDIOSO, (It.) } In a grand and elevated style.
GRAN GUSTO, (It.) }

GRAVAMENTE, (It.) Dignified and solemn.

GRAVE, (It.) The slowest degree of movement.

GRAVITA, (It.) Gravity; as, con gravita, with gravity.

GRAZIOSO, CON GRAZIA, (It.) Gracefully, elegantly.

GRUPPETTO, (It.) A group of notes; a turn.

GUSTO, GUSTOSO, or CON GUSTO, (It.) With taste, elegantly.

HALF-STFP. This term is used technically to denote the interval between the tones produced by any two contiguous keys of the Piano-forte.

HARMONY. The science of chords.

HOLD, (See PAUSE.)

IL, (It.) The.

IMITATION. This word is used technically to denote the response of one part to another in contrapuntal music.

IMPETUOSO, (It.) With impetuosity, impetuously.

IMPROMPTU, (Fr.)An extemporaneous production.

IMPROVISARE, (It.) To compose or sing extemporaneously.

IN, (It.) In; as, in tempo, in time.

INNOCENTE, INNOCENTEMENTE, (It.) In an artless and simple style.

INTERLUDE, (See § 95.)

INTERVAL. The difference of pitch between two tones.

INTRADA, } (It.) A short introductory
INTRODUZIONE } movement.

ISTESSO, (It.) The same; as, istesso tempo, the same time.

KEY. A lever pressed by the finger in playing an instrument. A system of tones, (See Chapter IV. Theo. Dept.)

LANGUENTE, } (It.) With languor.
LANGUIDO, }

LARGHETTO, (It.) Indicates a slow and measured movement, less so than largo.

LARGHISSIMO, (It.) A very slow and solemn degree of movement.

LEGATISSIMO, (It.) Very connectedly. The superlative of legato.

LEGATO, (It.) Connectedly. (See § 13, page 8.)

LEGEREMENT, (Fr.) With lightness and gayety.

LEGGIARDO, (It.) Light, gentle.

LEGGIERAMENTE, (It.) Lightly, gently.

LEGGIERO, or CON LEGGIEREZZA, (It.) With lightness and facility of execution.

LEGGIERISSIMO, (It.) With the utmost lightness and facility.

LENTANDO, (It.) With increasing slowness.

LENTEMENTE } (It.) In slow time.
LENTO, }

LIAISON, (Fr.) Smoothness of connection; also, a bind or tie.

LOCO, (Latin.) In the place. This word implies that a passage is to be played just as it is written in regard to pitch: it generally occurs after 8va alta, or 8va bassa.

MA, (It.) But; as, allegro ma non troppo, quick, but not too much so.

MAESTOSO, (It.) With majestic and dignified expression.

MAIN, (French.) The hand; as, main droite, main gauche, or M. D., M. G., the Right or Left hand in piano-forte music.

MAJOR, (Latin.) Large. This term is employed technically and distinctively in reference to intervals and keys. (See Chaps. VIII, IX and X, Theo. Dept.)

MANO, (It.) The hand. Mano dritta, the right hand; mano sinistra, the left hand.

MANUAL, (German.) The key-board.

MARCATISSIMO, (It.) In the most emphatic manner.

MARCATO, (It.) In a marked and emphatic style.

MARCHE, (French.) } A march.
MARCIA. (Italian.) }

MARQUEZ LES GROSSES NOTES, (French phrase.) Play the tones indicated by large notes louder and more distinctly than the others.

MARZIALE, (It.) In a martial style.

M. D. main droite, (French.) The right hand.

MELANGE, (Fr.) A composition founded on several favorite airs; a medley.

MEME, (Fr.) The same; as, meme movement, in the same time.

MENO, or MEN, (It.) Less; as, men presto, less quick; men forte, less loud; men piano, somewhat softer; meno vivo, with less spirit.

MESTO, (It.) Mournfully, sadly, pathetically.

MESTOSO, (It.) Sadly, pensively.

METRONOME, (Fr.) An ingenious instrument for indicating the exact time of a musical piece by means of a pendulum, which may be shortened or lengthened at pleasure.

MEZZO, (It.) In a middling degree or manner: as, mezzo forte, rather loud; mezzo piano, rather soft.

MEZZA VOCE, (It.) With moderation as to tone.

M. G. main gauche, (French.) The left hand.

MINOR, (Latin.) Small. This term is employed technically and distinctively in reference to intervals and keys. (See Chaps. VIII, IX and X, Theo. Dept.)

MINUETTO, (It.) A minuet: a slow dance in triple time.

MISERERE, (Lat.) A musical composition for the Romish Church, set to the 57th Psalm, beginning in Vulgate, miserere mei, domine.

MIT, (German.) With; as, mit begleitung, with an accompaniment.

MODERATO, (It.) With a moderate degree of quickness.

MOLTO, (It.) Very, extremely; as, molto allegro, very quick; molto adagio, extremely slow.

MORCEAU, (Fr.) A piece of musical composition of any kind.

MORDENTE, (It.) An embellishment differing from the double appoggiatura in accent only (see § 77.)

MORENDO, (It.) Gradually subsiding in regard to tone and time; dying away.

MOSSO, (It.) Movement; as, piu mosso, with more movement, quicker.

MOTIVO, (It.) See § 94.

MOTO, or CON MOTO, (It.) With agitation.

MOVIMENTO, (It.) Time, movement.

M. S. mano sinistra, (It.) The left hand.

NOBILE, } (It.) With nobleness, grandeur.
NOBILIMENTE, }

NON, (It.) An adverb of negation. generally associated with troppo: as non troppo presto, not too fast.

NOTTURNO, (It.) A composition, vocal or instrumental, of a plaintive character.

O, (It.) or, flauto o violino, flute or violin.

OBLIGATO, or OBLIGATI, (It.) A part or parts of a composition, indispensable to its just performance, and which, therefore, cannot properly be omitted.

OPERA, (It.) A dramatic composition set to music and sung on the stage, accompanied with musical instruments, and enriched with magnificent dresses, machines, dancing, &c.

OPUS, (Latin.) Work. (See note to page 68).

ORATORIO, (It.) A sacred musical composition consisting of airs, recitatives, choruses, &c., the subject of which is generally taken from scripture.

ORDINARIO, (It.) Usual: as, a tempo ordinario, in the usual time.

OTTAVA, or 8va (It.) An octave. This word is generally joined with alta or bassa; the first signifies that the passage to which it is applied must be played an octave higher than it is written; the second that it must be played an octave lower.

PASSIONATE, (It.) In an impassionate manner.

PASTORALE, (It.) A soft and rural movement.

PATETICO, (It.) Pathetically.

PATHÉTIQUE, (Fr.) Pathetic.

PAUSE, (It.) A character (⌒) indicating that a tone or silence may be prolonged at the pleasure of the performer.

PEDAL A CHAQUE MESURE, (French phrase.) Press the damper pedal at the beginning and allow it to rise at the close of every measure.

PERDENDO, PERDENDOSI, or PERDEN, (It.) implies a gradual diminution, both in the quantity of tone and speed of movement.

PEU, (Fr.) A little.

PHRASE, a short musical sentence containing an incomplete idea.

PIACERE, (It.) Will, pleasure; as, a piacere, at the performer's pleasure in regard to time.

PIANISSIMO, or pp, (It.) Extremely soft.

PIANO, or p, (It.) Soft.

PIU, (It.) An adverb of augmentation; as, piu presto, quicker; piu piano, softer.

PLANTIVO, (It.) Expressively, plaintively.

PLUS, (Fr.) More; as, plus anime, with greater animation.

POCO, (It.) A little, rather, somewhat; as, poco presto, rather quick; poco piano, somewhat soft.

POCO A POCO, (It.) By degrees, gradually; as, poco a poco crescendo, louder and louder by degrees; poco a poco diminuendo, softer and softer by degrees.

POI, (It.) Then; as, piano poi forte, soft, then loud.

POLLACCA, (It.) } A slow, Polish dance, in
POLONAISE, (Fr.) } 3-4 time, of a peculiar
POLONOISE, (Fr.) } rhythmical construction,
as the melodic members usually terminate on the third quarter of the measure.

POMPOSO, (It.) In a grand and pompous manner.

PORTAMENTO, (It.) The manner of sustaining and conducting the voice; a gliding from one note to another.

POSSIBILE, (It.) possible; as, piu forte possibile, as loud as possible.

POTPOURRI, (Fr.) A fantasia on favorite airs.

PRECIPITATO, (It.) In a hurried manner.

PRECISIONE, (It.) With precision, exactitude.

PRELUDIO, (It.) A prelude or introduction.

PREMIÈRE, (Fr.) First; as, première fois, first time.

PRESTEZZA, (It.) Rapidity, con prestezza possibile, with the utmost rapidity possible.

PRESTISSIMO, (It.) The most rapid degree of movement.

PRESTO, (It.) Very quick.

PRIMO, (It.) First; as, violino primo, first violin; tempo primo, in the first or original time.

QUADRILLE, (Fr.) A French dance.

QUASI, (It.) In the manner or style of; as, quasi allegretto, like an allegretto.

QUIETO, (It.) With calmness or repose; quietly.

RADDOLCENTE, } With augmented softness.
RADDOLCENTE, }

RALLENTANDO, (It.) Implies a gradual diminution in the speed of the movement, and a corresponding decrease in the quantity of tone.

RAPIDO, (It.) Rapidly.

RECITATIVO, (It.) A recitative or musical declamation.

RINFORZANDO, RINFORZATO, or *rinf*; or *rf.*, (*It.*) With additional tone and emphasis.

RISOLUTO, RISOLUMENTE, (*It.*) With boldness and resolution.

RITARDANDO, (*It.*) Moving slower and slower.

RITENENTE, RITENUTO, (*It.*) A keeping back, a decrease in the speed of the movement.

ROMANCE, (*It.*) } A short, lyric tale, set to music: ROMANZA, (*Fr.*) { or a simple and elegant melody suitable to such words.

RONDEAU, (*Fr.*) } A rondo or composition of sev-
RONDO, (*It.*) { eral strains or members, at the end of each of which the first part or subject is repeated.

RONDINO, RONDILETTA, RONDINETTO, or RONDOLETTO, (*It.*) A short rondo.

ROOT. The fundamental note of any chord. (See § 177.)

SCHERZANDO, SCHERZANTE, SCHERZOSO, or SCHERZ, (*It.*) In a light, playful, and sportive manner.

SEGNO, or 𝄋, (*It.*) A sign; as, *al segno*, return to the sign; *dal segno*, repeat from the sign.

SEGUE, SEGUITO, (*It.*) Now follows; or, as follows; as, *segue il coro*, the chorus follows; *segue la finale*, the *finale* now follows. It is also used in the sense of, *in similar* or *like manner*, to show that a subsequent passage is to be played like that which precedes it.

SEMITONE. This word is used technically to denote the interval between the tones produced by any two contiguous keys of the Piano-forte. (See Half-step.)

SEMPLICE, SEMPLICEMENTE, (*It.*) With simplicity, artlessly.

SEMPRE, (*It.*) Always; as, *sempre staccato*, always staccato or detached; *sempre forte*, always loud; *sempre più forte*, continually increasing in force.

SENZA, (*It.*) Without; as *senza organo*, without the organ; *senza rigore*, without regard to exact time; *senza replica*, without repetition.

SERIOSO, (*It.*) In serious style.

SERPEGGIANDO, (*It.*) Gently and silently creeping onwards, quietly advancing.

SFORZATO, SFORZANDO, or *sf.* (*It.*) Implies that a particular note is to be played with emphasis.

SHAKE. A trill.

SICILIANA, (*It.*) A movement of a slow, soothing, pastoral character, in 6-8 time, resembling a dance peculiar to the peasantry of Sicily.

SINFONIA, (*It.*) A symphony or orchestral composition in many parts.

SINISTRA, (*It.*) The left hand.

SLENTANDO, (*It.*) A gradual diminution in the time or speed of the movement.

SMORZANDO, (*It.*) A gradual diminution as to tone.

SOAVE, (*It.*) In a soft, sweet, and delicate style.

SOGGETTO, (*It.*) The subject or theme.

SOLI, *plural of* SOLO, (*It.*) Implies that two or more principal parts play or sing together. Such parts, of course, are never doubled.

SOLO, SOLA, (*It.*) Alone.

SOLO, (*It.*) A composition, or even a passage, for a single voice or instrument.

SONATA, *It.*) } A composition consisting of sev-
SONATE, (*Fr.*) { eral principal instrument, with or without ac-single principal instrument, with or without accompaniments.

SOSTENUTO, or SOST, (*It.*) Sustained, continuous in regard to tone.

SOTTO VOCE, (*It.*) In an under tone.

SPIRITO, CON SPIRITO, (*It.*) With spirit.

SPIRITOSO, (*It.*) With great spirit.

STACCATO, (*It.*) Implies that tones are to be distinct, detached from one another.

STEP. This term is used technically to denote the interval between the tones produced by any key of the Piano-forte and the next key but one to the right of it, black or white.

SUBITO, (*It.*) Quickly; as, *volti subito*, turn quickly.

SUITE, (*Fr.*) A series, a collection; as, *une suite de pièces*, a series of lessons.

SYNCOPATE, (*It.*) In a constrained and syncopated style.

SYNCOPATION, (*It.*) See § 107.

TANTO, NON, (*It.*) Not so much; not too much.

TARDO, (*It.*) Slowly, in a dragging manner.

TEMA, (*It.*) A melody.

TEMPESTOSO, (*It.*) In a tempestuous manner.

TEMPO or A TEMPO, (*It.*) In time. An expression used after some relaxation in the measure, to indicate a return to the original movement.

TEMPO COMODO, (*It.*) In a convenient degree of movement.

TEMPO GIUSTO, (*It.*) In strict time.

TEMPO PRIMO, (*It.*) In the first or original time.

TENDREMENT, (*Fr.*) Affectionately, tenderly.

TENERAMENTE, TENERO, or CON TENEREZ-ZA, (*It.*) Tenderly.

TIMOROSO, (*It.*) With timidity, awe.

TONE. A musical sound. This word is also used technically, though improperly, to denote the interval of a step.

TRANQUILLO, TRANQUILLAMENTE, or CON TRANQUILLEZZA, (*It.*) Tranquilly, composedly.

TREMANDO, } (*It.*) Implies the reiteration of a
TREMOLATE, } tone or chord with great rapidity,
TREMOLO, } so as to produce a tremulous kind of motion.

TREMENDO, (*It.*) With a tremendous expression, horribly.

TRILLANDO, (*It.*) A succession of trills.

TRIO, (*It.*) A piece for three voices or instruments. This term also denotes a second movement to a waltz, march, minuet, &c. which always leads back to a repetition of the first or principal movement.

TRIPLET, a group of three notes, performed in the time usually occupied by two of the same kind.

TUTTA FORZA, (*It.*) With the utmost vehemence, as loud as possible.

TUTTI, (*It.* plural, all.) A term used to point out those passages where all the voices or instruments, or both, are to be introduced.

TRILL. An embellishment consisting of a rapid alternation of two tones at the interval of a second. (See §§ 48 and 77.)

UN, (*It.*) A; as, *un poco*, a little.

VALCE, (*It.*) } A waltz.
VALSE, (*Fr.*) }

VELOCE, or CON VELOCITA, (*It.*) In rapid time.

VELOCISSIMO, (*It.*) In extreme rapidity.

VIGOROSO, VIGOROSAMENTE, (*It.*) Boldly, vigorously.

VISTAMENTE, (*It.*) } With quickness.
VITE, (*Fr.*) }

VIVACE, VIVAMENTE, or CON VIVACITA, (*It.*) With briskness and animation.

VIVACISSIMO, (*It.*) With extreme vivacity.

VIVACITA, (*It.*) Vivacity.

VIVO, CON VIVEZZA, (*It.*) Animated, lively.

VOCE, (*It.*) The voice.

VOLANTE, (*It.*) In a light and rapid manner.

VOLTA, (*It.*) Time of playing a movement; as, *prima volta*, the first time of playing, &c.

VOLTI SUBITO, or V. S., (*It.*) Turn over quickly.

WALZER, (*Ger.*) A Waltz.

ZEFFIROSO, (*It.*) Zephyr-like. *Con leggierezza quasi zeffiroso*, In a light and airy manner, like a gentle breeze.

INDEX.

Abbreviation...........................56, 68
Accent Exercises, upon Two Tones............151
" " upon Three Tones.............153
" " " Four Tones..............154
" " " Five Tones........147, 151, 155
" " " Chromatic Scale....157, 167, 212
" " " Diatonic Scale.........168, 194
" " " Broken Chords.........165, 193
" " " Arpeggios............194, 209
" " " Broken Thirds and Sixths, 210, 211
" " " Octaves.............212, 214
Accent Studies.......................216, 219
Accentuation, importance of...............146
" principles of, § 80...............146
" Suggestions to Teachers..........147
Accompaniments of vocal music..............82
Action Pedal................................68
"Allegro" by Baryiel, Op. 33..............117
American fingering...........................8
"Amoroso," Egghard.........................110
Analysis of fingering.....84, 25, 46, 66, 68, 234
Analysis of tones..........................226
"Andante" by Czerny, Op. 359...............96
"Andante" by Mozart........................143
"Andante" from "William Tell"..............72
Appoggiaturas..........................86, 131
Broken Triads...................56, 165, 191
" " Chords of Dominant Seventh......192
" " " Diminished Seventh......193
Chromatic Octaves......................87, 212
Chromatic Scale.........17, 157, 167, 212, 228, 234
Celerity, how to acquire it.................71
"Cradle Song," Schumann...................119
Damper Pedal................................68
"Desire," Waltz.............................80
"Don Pasquale" Fantaisie....................89
Double Appoggiatura........................131
Double-sixth Scales...................124, 211
Double-third Scales...................102, 210
Dynamic force, training for.................71
Dynamics...................................221
Exercise No. 1..............................7
" " 2 and 8................................8
" " 4 " 6................................9
" " 6....................................10
" " 7....................................12
" " 8....................................13
" " 9, Chromatic Scale....... 18
" " 10, Diatonic Scale....................19
" " 11, First Class of Major Scales.......20
" " 12, do. Contrary motion..............24
" " 13, To be fingered...................26
" " 14, Second Class Major Scales........28
" " 15, Third Class Major Scales.........32
" " 16, Extensions.......................33
" " 17, Review of Scales.................39
" " 18 and 19............................40
" " 20, The hand moved by extension, 42
" " 21, " " " contraction, 45
" " 22, Thirds.......................47, 49
" " 23, Repitition by change of fingers, 49

Exercise No. 24, Repetition by the same finger...50
" " 25, " " action of wrist... 52
" " 26, Trill Study.......................54
" " 27, Broken Triads.....................56
" " 28, First Class Minor Scales..........58
" " 29, Second " " "...............59
" " 30, Third " " "................60
" " 31, Preparation for Arpeggios.... 62
" " 32, Octave Study......................64
" " 33, Wrist Study.......................75
" " 34, Sixths, legato....................82
" " 35, Vocal accompaniments.............82
" " 36, " 84
" " 37, Chromatic Octaves in alternation...........................87
" " 38, "Study," Heller, Op. 46. No. 1..98
" " 39, "Study," Heller, Op. 46. No. 3..100
" " 40, Double Third Scales..............102
" " 41, " Sixth " 194
" " 42 to 55, Inclusive, Interlocking Passages...................134, 142
" " 56 to 228, Accent Exercises..147, 214
" " 229, Trill Exercise.................215
False and true methods of Teaching...........5
"Fantaisie" from "Don Pasquale"...........89
Fingering, theory of......................234
First Class Major Scales....................20
" " Minor Scales.........................58
Flexibility..................................5
Four parts, arrangement of..................62
General Practice............................71
General Rules for fingering................234
Hands, how held........................6, 11
Hands, how moved......................42, 45
Hands in Arpeggios..........................62
Harmony...............................231, 233
"Haus-Musik," Reinecke...................109
"Home, sweet home".......................101
"If I were a bird," Henselt...............126
Improvisation........................226, 234
Instrument, importance of....................6
Interlocking passages..................133, 142
Interludes.................................223
Intervals..............................228, 229
Learning difficult pieces...................71
"Le Rossignol"..............................60
Major Scales.........19, 21, 22, 27, 28, 33, 39
" Accent Exercises...........168, 184
"Mazurka," Chopin, Op. 7, No. 5............60
Melodics...............................226, 231
Measurement of time......................9, 43
"Melody and Scale":........................97
Melodies from "Martha"....................66
"Menuetto and Trio," Schubert............122
Minor Scales.......................58, 60, 230, 232
Minute counting............................43
"Miserere" from "Trovatore"..............104
Mordent, the..............................132
"Night's shade no longer".................126
Notation..............................235, 230
Notation of complicated passages..........86

Passages, classes of......................234
Playing at sight...........................83
Playing for listeners......................71
"Prelude," Chopin, Op. 28, No. 7...........80
" " " 20.............102
Preparation for the Trill...................52
" Polka Mazurka," Ladus...................76
Practice, general directions...............71
Recreations, First and Second..............10
" Third.................................12
" Fourth and Fifth......................14
" Sixth.................................15
" Seventh...............................16
" Eighth................................17
" Ninth.................................19
" Tenth.................................20
" Eleventh..............................22
" Twelfth...............................24
" Thirteenth............................25
" Fourteenth............................30
" Fifteenth.............................31
" Sixteenth and Seventeenth.............32
" Eighteenth............................33
" Nineteenth............................55
" Twentieth and Twenty-first............56
" Twenty-second and Twenty-third........87
" Twenty-fourth.........................38
" Twenty-fifth..........................41
" Twenty-sixth..........................42
" Twenty-seventh........................43
" Twenty-eighth.........................48
" Twenty-ninth..........................50
" Thirtieth.............................52
" Thirty-first..........................57
" Thirty-second.........................62
" Thirty-third..........................54
Rhythmics.............................225, 226
Scales, Chromatic......................17, 18
" " Accent Exercises..157, 167, 212
" in Double Thirds..................102, 210
" in Double Sixths..................124, 211
" Major...19, 21, 22, 24, 27, 28, 33, 39, 228, 234
" " Accent Exercises..........164, 168
" Minor.................58, 60, 230, 234
Second Class of Major Scales................28
Second Class Minor Scales...................59
"Serenade," Schubert......................114
Sixths.........................82, 134, 211, 234
"Slumber Song," Heller...................106
Staccato touch.........................40, 42
Studies, remarks upon.......................52
"The Desire," Waltz........................80
Theoretical Department....................225
Theory of fingering.......................234
Third Class Major Scales....................32
Third Class Minor Scales....................60
Thirds.........................47, 210, 234
Triads.....................56, 165, 194, 231, 236
Wrist Study.................................75

www.ingramcontent.com/pod-product-compliance
Lightning Source LLC
Chambersburg PA
CBHW030406270326
41926CB00009B/1296